Dating

Dating

Other Books of Related Interest

Teen Decisions Series
Pregnancy
Sex

Opposing Viewpoints Series
Abortion
Adoption
Human Sexuality
Sex
Teenage Pregnancy
Teenage Sexuality
Teens at Risk

Current Controversies Series
The Abortion Controversy
Gay Rights
Sexually Transmitted Diseases
Teen Pregnancy and Parenting

Contemporary Issues Companions
Teen Pregnancy
Teens and Sex

At Issue Series
Date Rape
The Ethics of Abortion
Sex Education
Sexually Transmitted Diseases
Teen Sex

Dating

Jennifer A. Hurley, *Book Editor*

Daniel Leone, *President*
Bonnie Szumski, *Publisher*
Scott Barbour, *Managing Editor*

Teen
Decisions

Greenhaven Press Inc., San Diego, California

646.7

No part of this book may be reproduced or used in any form or by any means, electrical, mechanical, or otherwise, including, but not limited to, photocopy, recording, or any information storage and retrieval system, without prior written permission from the publisher.

Every effort has been made to trace owners of copyrighted material.

Library of Congress Cataloging-in-Publication Data

Dating / Jennifer A. Hurley, book editor.
    p. cm. — (Teen decisions)
    Includes bibliographical references and index.
    ISBN 0-7377-0920-0 (pbk. : alk. paper) —
    ISBN 0-7377-0921-9 (lib. bdg. : alk. paper)
    1. Dating (Social customs) I. Hurley, Jennifer A., 1973– .

HQ801 .D335 2002
646.7'7—dc21   2001040611
                                                                   CIP

Cover photo: © Steve Thornton/Corbis

© 2002 by Greenhaven Press, Inc.
10911 Technology Place, San Diego, CA 92127

Printed in the U.S.A.

Contents

Foreword

The teen years are a time of transition from childhood to adulthood. By age 13, most teenagers have started the process of physical growth and sexual maturation that enables them to produce children of their own. In the United States and other industrialized nations, teens who have entered or completed puberty are still children in the eyes of the law. They remain the responsibility of their parents or guardians and are not expected to make major decisions themselves. In most of the United States, eighteen is the age of legal adulthood. However, in some states, the age of majority is nineteen, and some legal restrictions on adult activities, such as drinking alcohol, extend until age twenty-one.

This prolonged period between the onset of puberty and the achieving of legal adulthood is not just a matter of hormonal and physical change, but a learning process as well. Teens must learn to cope with influences outside the immediate family. For many teens, friends or peer groups become the basis for many of their opinions and actions. In addition, teens are influenced by TV shows, advertising, and music.

The *Teen Decisions* series aims at helping teens make responsible choices. Each book provides readers with thought-provoking advice and information from a variety of perspectives. Most of the articles in these anthologies were originally written for, and in many cases by, teens. Some of the essays focus on ethical and moral dilemmas, while others present pertinent legal and scientific information. Many of the articles tell personal stories about decisions teens have made and how their lives were affected.

One special feature of this series is the "Points of Contention," in which specially paired articles present directly opposing views on controversial topics. Additional features in each book include a listing of organizations to contact for more information, as well as a bibliography to aid readers interested in more information. The *Teen Decisions* series strives to include both trustworthy information and multiple opinions on topics important to teens, while respecting the role teens play in making their own choices.

Introduction

"I've practiced the opening lines 'til I know them by heart," says Dave, an American high school student. "But I've never asked any girl out on a date—because you need more than opening lines. There's a whole evening when you've got to find something to talk about."[1] Dave's anxiety about dating is typical of many teens' views in the United States today. Like Dave, numerous adolescents are eager to begin dating, but they perhaps lack the self-esteem or social skills needed to help them make the leap into the dating arena. Many other teens, however, are perfectly comfortable with the prospect of dating. One female senior says, for example, "There is emphasis in this school to have a steady date. This is not a problem for me. For those who don't have a lot of self-esteem, there may be more pressure, like to have sex."[2] This young woman, and other teens like her, has enough confidence to handle any dating dilemma.

Most teens' views about dating fall likely somewhere between these two extremes. Every teen is probably nervous about the prospect of dating for the first time. All teens must struggle to decide when they are ready to begin dating. The truth is there are no set rules about dating that can apply to every teen everywhere. This fact can make dating an exciting, liberating experience, but it can also make the decision to start dating a scary one.

Dating also requires a degree of maturity and responsibility that may seem a little scary to some adolescents. Teens must develop time-management skills in order to balance dating with their studies, sports activities, and other extracurricular duties at school or in the community. Next, people who date have to make mature decisions about whether to see more than one person at once, learning to be careful not to double-book dates if they do decide to play the field. Dating also requires teens to develop social skills by making good on promises to call people, returning calls, and learning to politely refuse dates from people they do not want to go out with. Finally, there are a lot of expenses involved in dating. Budgeting for dates is difficult on an allowance, so many teens have jobs that can help them afford dinners out, movies, theme parks, dance clubs, and other venues.

Deciding whether or not to have sex is another adult responsibility that may arise when adolescents begin dating. While many teens who date decide to become sexually active, others decide to wait and have sex when they are older or in a committed relationship. When you are dating, you may find yourself in sexually charged situations, such as being alone with someone who is pressuring you for sex. There are also potentially dangerous risks associated with dating: teens can just as easily fall victim as adults to date rape and relationship violence.

Deciding When to Date

While there are a lot of questions to think about and some dangers to be aware of, dating is a pretty natural act for most American teens. How old should a teen be before he or she starts dating? Some teens look to their culture, community, or parents, who may have already set up some guidelines that they expect teens to follow, but ultimately teens themselves are the best people to decide when they are ready to start dating. Some teens feel ashamed or awkward if their brothers or sisters began dating at age sixteen while they still feel more comfortable just hanging around with groups of friends at that age. Others also feel pressured by their friends to date. "Only start dating when you want to and not because others are doing it," says Peggy Brick, president of the Sexuality Information and Education Council of the United States (SIECUS). "There's a lot of peer pressure and many people begin dating before they really want to."[3]

Daniel Lopez is a fourteen-year-old boy who says he's decided to put off dating because he has seen a lot of his friends get hurt from dating too soon. "What happens when you date, a little piece of you tends to go with every person and less of you stays with you," he says. "A little piece of your heart and soul and mind is scattered all over the place."[4] Worried that dating would distract him from his other priorities, Daniel prefers to go out with his friends for the time being. Thirteen-year-old Addison Brown, on the other hand, claims to have been going out with girls since the fourth grade. "Dating makes you feel great about yourself, but breaking up or not dating can hurt, too," Addison says. "When you're dating, you just think, 'Hey, I'm with a girl.' If you're not dating, it's kind of like a bummer. It's like you got this thing tied around your neck that says, 'Hey, you're a loser.'"[5] In short, being ready to date has little to do with age, or whether friends are dating, and everything to do with how teens are starting to feel about potential dating partners.

Deciding Who to Date

If a teenager is feeling ready to start dating but does not already have someone special in mind, he or she will likely begin to spend a lot of time thinking about who *is* available for dating. Unless teens have jobs or participate in extracurricular activities that allow them to meet a wide range of people, they will most likely meet and date boys or girls who attend the same school or live in the same neighborhood. From this pool, teens already know a lot of people, but they begin to look at these people differently as they size them up as potential dating material.

As in deciding when to date, deciding who to date comes down to gauging who teens are most comfortable with. The key is not to date anyone, male or female, who you feel will pressure you into doing things you are not ready for (like drinking or becoming sexually active). For this reason, many teens try to date others who are as close to their own age and level of maturity as possible and who share similar interests and values as their own.

America's high schools are increasingly becoming as diverse demographically as America itself. This fact increases teens' chances of meeting (and dating) people from a wide range of ethnicities and religious backgrounds. Dating someone with a different cultural upbringing than yourself may not seem problematic to many teens, but even in the new millennium, interracial or interfaith dating can be controversial, especially if you live in a community that expects you to date within your own race or religion. Authors Nancy and Robert Kolodny and Thomas Bratter write that when dating someone with a fundamentally different ethnic or religious background than your own, "the sad truth is that life can be made very hard for you and your date . . . —you can practically count on hearing racial slurs, people may question your sanity and values, and you may be ostracized from your family and prior social group." Nevertheless, the authors contend that who teens choose to date is ultimately up to them. "If the disadvantages [of interracial or interfaith dating] don't outweigh the advantages, go ahead and begin to date," the authors suggest.

> The bottom line is that you're two people who really like each other and enjoy each other's company. Even if the disadvantages seem horrendous, you may decide to encourage the relationship. It *is* possible that together you can overcome people's preconceived ideas. It's also possible that your dating won't cause any problems at all. But you'll never know until you try, and you may live to regret it if you don't try.[6]

Same-Sex Dating

Like teens who decide to date outside their race or religion, homosexual teens may face special hurdles when they decide to "come out" to their friends and families and date same-sex partners openly. According to one study at the Hetrick Martin Institute in New York, 80 percent of homosexual or bisexual adolescents reported feeling isolated from their peers and family. Feeling cut off from one's peers certainly affects one's self-esteem and limits opportunities to make friends or meet dating partners. In addition to feeling isolated, gay and lesbian teens often suffer harsh treatment by others. Twenty-three percent of lesbian teens, for example, experience verbal or physical abuse while at school. In this light, the decision to date is especially difficult for the majority of gay and lesbian teens who come out to peers, parents, or communities not accepting of homosexual lifestyles.

In communities that are accepting of gay and lesbian citizens, homosexual teens may not worry too much about declaring their same-sex preference. These teens, like their heterosexual peers, will simply suffer the more everyday anxieties about asking people out, wondering where to go on dates, and deciding what to wear. Yoshima, a lesbian teen from Seattle, was surprised when she finally came out to her family and they told her that they always knew she was homosexual. Since she was already dating someone at the time, she says, "Coming out didn't have a huge impact for me socially, but it did personally. It was the first time in my life that I actually felt comfortable being a woman. Coming out made me realize I was OK as a person and as a woman."[7]

Sex and Dating

No matter who teens decide to date, once they begin dating, they will probably begin to think about whether they are also ready to become sexually active. Just because a young man or woman is dating, however, does not necessarily mean that he or she is ready to have sexual relations. But once teens start dating, sex *will* become an issue.

As in deciding whether you are ready to start dating, only you can decide whether you are ready to become physically involved with someone. Some adolescents feel that having sex is no big deal, while others have reported that they wished they had held off on having sex until they were older. Fourteen-year-old Rick, for example, feels he was surprised into deciding to have sex too soon:

I was making out with this girl Katrina. We had just started seeing each other. Suddenly she's all over me, trying to take my clothes off. I froze. I wasn't expecting her to be so aggressive. I really hadn't even thought about sex with her, or with anyone. I figured I was still too young. Boy, did she take me by surprise. The worst part was, she made me feel really stupid for hesitating, as if the guy is supposed to want to do it all the time.[8]

While Rick felt comfortable kissing Katrina, he clearly was not ready to have sex with her.

Many sociologists warn that teens not only need to be emotionally prepared for sex, but also need to be knowledgeable about protection against pregnancy and sexually transmitted diseases, like AIDS, as well. Some suggest that teens postpone having sex until they and their partners are ready to assume the responsibility of protecting themselves against these occurrences. The authors of *Finding Our Way* advise, "Unless you're going to use contraception, including a condom, correctly, *every time you have sex* to protect yourself against pregnancy and sexually transmitted infections, WAIT."[9]

Dating Danger: Some Dates End in Date Rape

If you decide not to have sexual relations while dating—whether you define sex as kissing, petting, oral sex, or having intercourse—in most cases you can expect that your wishes will be respected by your dates. Jeremy Daldry, author of *The Teenage Guy's Survival Guide,* warns, however, that boys and girls have different expectations about dating that can be potentially harmful. "Girls expect this romantic encounter," he says, "while boys sometimes hope for a sexual encounter much like what they see on TV."[10] Because of these differing expectations, young women, especially, should be aware that numerous teens each year are the victims of acquaintance, or date, rape. According to the National Victim Center, by 1995 over 12 million American women had been raped, and most of these victims were between the ages of eleven and seventeen.[11] And nearly twice as many women are raped each year by people they know—such as someone they are on a date with—than are raped by strangers. While women are most often the victims of rape, young men can be victims as well. Rape can be defined as unwanted sexual contact; intercourse does not have to occur for a sexual assault to have taken place. Many teens do not speak up after they have been date raped because they feel ashamed of the activities that occurred or believe they are somehow responsible for the rape.

Fortunately, there are steps teens can take to help protect themselves against becoming victims of date rape. First, experts suggest that teens don't do anything that can impair their decision-making abilities while on a date, such as drinking or taking drugs. Studies show that 75 percent of men and 55 percent of women claim to have been drinking or taking drugs when an acquaintance rape occurred.[12] Accepting drinks of any kind (even soda) from dates can even be dangerous if you did not see the drink being poured—drugging drinks is a common tactic among would-be rapists.

Even if teens are careful to remain drug and alcohol free on dates, they still need to be careful not to go anywhere with their dates that could compromise their safety. Criminologists warn that until you get to know someone well enough to trust them, only go out with them to public places, like well-populated movie theaters (not the drive-in!) and restaurants. Certainly do not allow your date to take you anywhere that is secluded from the public, as many acquaintance rapes occur in remote locations.

An Alternative to One-on-One Dating

Often teens feel ready to start dating, but they are worried about warding off unwanted sexual advances from dates, or they are just nervous about how to act on a date. These teens might consider group dating before going out with someone alone. They are probably already used to going out with groups of friends, so going out with a group of couples could feel very natural to them. Psychologist Susan Goodman agrees that group dating is a good way for adolescents to warm up to the idea of going on dates alone. "Once you hit a certain age," Goodman writes, "members of the opposite sex seem more like members of an entirely different species—and just as scary. . . . Group dating is a great way to bring the opposite sex back into the human race. After several outings, they start to seem like people again, albeit people somewhat different from you."[13]

In addition to learning how to work out nervousness and become comfortable around the opposite sex, Goodman notes, group dating will ultimately help teens hone their social skills. Adolescents can watch how their peers carry on conversations and learn from their successes and foibles. They can build up confidence in this manner as they "experiment with when to take a leadership role or the backseat [in group conversations] and how to entertain others and be entertained."[14]

Finally, group dating has the added benefit of putting parents at ease about teen dating, or even offering them a way to compromise if they feel their sons or daughters are still too young to be dating at all. As Goodman notes, when teens date in groups parents "are willing to give their children new privileges—later curfews, a new range of evening activities—because they see a group as lending safety through its numbers."[15]

Deciding to Date Will Change Relationships at Home

Whether you choose to go on group dates or go out alone with your dates, the fact that you are dating at all is bound to change your relationship with your parents. Your dating is a clear sign to your parents that you are growing up—a fact that may alternately both worry and excite them. You may not even be old enough to drive yet, but once you start dating, they will feel they are losing you to the adult world.

Authors Bonnie B. Dowdy and Wendy Kliewer explain the new

tense feelings that might arise at home when teens begin to date: "In dating relationships, adolescents experience themselves in a role different than that of child, student, or friend. Parents, however, continue to experience the adolescent living at home and going to school as still a child."[16]

These differences in perception can lead to increased conflict. As adolescents explore their new role in the dating scene, it is likely that their priorities about homework and family life will change. Parents, however, will have the same expectations they have always had about these issues. In addition, while teens enjoy their newfound freedom, "parents may want to increase control due to the risks they feel are associated with dating. These multiple changes can result in new, renewed, or increased frequency or intensity of conflict over the mundane matters, as well as over dating per se."[17]

The point here is that families worry about adolescents once they decide to start dating. If you keep the lines of communication about your dating experiences open with your parents, allow them to meet your dates, and respect the curfews they set for you, you are bound to lessen some of their feelings of anxiety about your dating.

Deciding About Dating

Dating is a rite of passage in our society that most teens will participate in. Going out on dates with one person or many people during the teen years is a way of transitioning from the play dates of childhood into more adult relationships. With that transition, however, also come adult responsibilities that make the decision to date an important and often difficult one. The essays collected in *Teen Decisions: Dating* will help you think about dating from a variety of perspectives. Teen authors talk frankly about their own positive and negative dating experiences, discussing how their decisions to date or not date have affected their lives. Adult dating and relationship experts also discuss the benefits and potential dangers of dating.

In chapter 1, "Deciding Who and When to Date," you will find insight about dating your friends, dating more than one person at once, and choosing not to date at all. Chapter 2, "Dating Problems," discusses the difficult moments inherent in dating that most teens will experience, such as breakups and unrequited love. This chapter also further highlights some of the dangers of dating like acquaintance rape and abusive relationships, important issues that all teens thinking about dating should be aware of. Finally, chapter 3, "Dating and Sex," brings teens' feelings about sex and dating out in the open. As you will see, both male and female teens talk here about taking pride in their virginity. Other teens who have made the decision to have sex discuss the unexpected pitfalls of becoming sexually active. A nationally recognized founder of an online sexuality resource site for teens offers advice for measuring your material, physical, and emotional readiness for sex. In all, the essays in *Teen Decisions: Dating* provide a good introduction to some different perspectives on teen dating that will help you responsibly decide if dating, right now, is right for you.

Notes

1. Quoted in Susan Goodman, "Group Dating: Safety in Numbers," *Current Health 2,* December 1987, p. 12.
2. Quoted in Eileen Kalberg VanWie, *Teenage Stress: How to Cope in a Complex World.* New York: Julian Messner, 1987, p. 50.
3. Quoted in Allison Abner and Linda Villarosa, *Finding Our Way: The Teen Girl's Survival Guide.* New York: HarperPerennial, 1995, p. 237.
4. Quoted in Farah Fleurima, "Not Quite Ready for Romance," *Dallas Morning News,* March 3, 2000, pp. 1C–2C.
5. Quoted in Fleurima, "Not Quite Ready for Romance," p. 1C.
6. Nancy J. Kolodny et al., *Smart Choices.* Boston: Little, Brown, 1986, p. 123.
7. Quoted in Abner and Villarosa, *Finding Our Way,* p. 251.
8. Quoted in Diane Kolyer, *Everything You Need to Know About Dating.* New York: Rosen, 1991, p. 50.
9. Abner and Villarosa, *Finding Our Way,* p. 243.
10. Quoted in Fleurima, "Not Quite Ready for Romance," p. 1C.
11. Abner and Villarosa, *Finding Our Way,* p. 274.

12. Abner and Villarosa, *Finding Our Way*, p. 274.

13. Goodman, "Group Dating," p. 12.

14. Goodman, "Group Dating," p. 13.

15. Goodman, "Group Dating," p. 13.

16. Bonnie B. Dowdy and Wendy Kliewer, "Dating: Parent-Adolescent Conflict, and Behavioral Autonomy," *Journal of Youth and Adolescence*, August 1998, p. 20.

17. Dowdy and Kliewer, "Dating," p. 20.

Chapter 1

Deciding Who and When to Date

Teen
Decisions

I Kissed Dating Goodbye

Joshua Harris

Most teens take it for granted that they will date quite a few people before they make the lifelong commitment of marriage. Joshua Harris, on the other hand, has decided to do otherwise. After making several weighty promises to girls that he couldn't fulfill, Harris made the decision to stop dating entirely. In this excerpt from his book *I Kissed Dating Goodbye,* he explains how he came to the realization that dating is harmful—to his own emotional health, to the girls he cared about, and to his relationship with God.

It was finally here—Anna's wedding day, the day she had dreamed about and planned for months. The small, picturesque church was crowded with friends and family. Sunlight poured through the stained-glass windows, and the gentle music of a stringed quartet filled the air. Anna walked down the aisle toward David. Joy surged within her. This was the moment for which she had waited so long. He gently took her hand, and they turned toward the altar.

But as the minister began to lead Anna and David through their vows, the unthinkable happened. A girl stood up in the middle of the congregation, walked quietly to the altar, and took David's other hand. Another girl approached and stood next to the first, followed by another. Soon, a chain of six girls stood by him as he repeated his vows to Anna.

Anna felt her lip beginning to quiver as tears welled up in her eyes. "Is this some kind of joke?" she whispered to David.

"I'm . . . I'm sorry, Anna," he said, staring at the floor.

"Who are these girls, David? What is going on?" she gasped.

"They're girls from my past," he answered sadly. "Anna, they don't mean anything to me now . . . but I've given part of my heart to each of them."

"I thought your heart was mine," she said.

"It is, it is," he pleaded. "Everything that's left is yours."

A tear rolled down Anna's cheek. Then she woke up.

Betrayed

Anna told me about her dream in a letter. "When I awoke I felt so betrayed," she wrote. "But then I was struck with this sickening thought: How many men could line up next to *me* on my wedding day? How many times have I given my heart away in short-term relationships? Will I have anything left to give my husband?"

I often think of Anna's dream. The jarring image haunts me. There are girls from my past, too. What if they showed up on my wedding day? What could they say in the receiving line?

> While dating, I made many decisions based on superficiality and ignorance.

"Hello, Joshua. Those were some pretty lofty promises you made at the altar today. I hope you're better at keeping promises now than you were when I knew you."

"My, don't you look nice in that tuxedo. And what a beautiful bride. Does she know about me? Have you told her all the sweet things you used to whisper in *my* ear?"

There are relationships that I can only look back on with regret. I do my best to forget. I laugh them off as part of the game of love that everyone plays. I know God has forgiven me be-cause I've asked Him to. I know the various girls have forgiven me because I've asked them to.

But I still feel the ache of having given away my heart to too many girls in my past.

That's Just the Way It Is

Growing up, I considered dating an essential part of the com-plete teenage experience. If I wasn't dating a girl, I had a crush on one.

This started in junior high when my peers and I treated dating as a game, a chance to play at love and experiment with rela-tionships. Having a girlfriend meant little more than saying you were "going out." No big deal. My friends and I would go out with girls and break up with them at a frightening pace. The only worry was being dumped—you never wanted to *get* dumped, you wanted to *do* the dumping. One girl I knew had the fastest breakup routine ever: When she was ready to end a relationship, she'd say, "Skippy-bop, you just got dropped."

But soon, just saying you were going out with someone wasn't enough. Instead, we began experimenting with the phys-ical side of relationships. Going out with someone came to mean you made out with that person, too. I remember standing by as a girl I liked called her boyfriend and broke up with him over the phone. As soon as she hung up, she kissed me. That meant we were an "official couple." Looking back, I can only shake my head at how immature we were. The physical intimacy of those junior high relationships had nothing to do with love or real af-fection. We just mimicked what we saw older kids do and what we watched in the movies. It seemed grown up, but in reality it was lust.

I'm thankful that junior high didn't last forever. In high school, I got serious about my walk with God and became actively in-volved in the church youth group. I put an "I'm Worth Waiting

For" sticker on my NIV Student Bible and promised to stay a virgin until I got married. Unfortunately, youth group did little to improve my immature notions about relationships. Even in church we played the dating game with passion—more passion, I regret to say, than we gave to worshiping or listening to sermons. During Sunday morning services we passed notes about who liked whom, who was going out with whom, and who had broken up with whom. Wednesday night youth group meetings served as our own opportunities to play "Love Connection," a game that resulted in broken hearts littering the foyer.

My First Girlfriend

In my sophomore year, my involvement in the dating game took a more serious turn. That summer, I met Kelly. She was beautiful, blonde, and two inches taller than I. I didn't mind. Kelly was popular, and all the guys liked her. Since I was the only one in the youth group who had the nerve to talk to her, she wound up liking me. I asked her to be my girlfriend on the youth group's water ski retreat.

Kelly was my first serious girlfriend. Everyone in our youth group recognized us as a couple. We celebrated our "anniversary" every month. And Kelly knew me better than anyone else. After my folks were asleep, Kelly and I would spend hours on the phone, often late into the night, talking about everything and nothing in particular. We thought God had made us for each other. We talked about getting married someday. I promised her that I would love her forever.

But, like many high school relationships, our romance was premature—too much, too soon. We began to struggle with the physical side of our relationship. We knew we couldn't be as close physically as we were emotionally. As a result, we experienced ongoing tension, and it wore on us. Eventually, things turned sour.

"We have to break up," I said to her one night after a movie. We both knew this was coming.

"Is there any chance we can have something in the future?" she asked.

"No," I said, trying to add resolve to my voice. "No, it's over."

We broke up two years after we'd met. Not quite "forever," as I had promised.

Something Better

I was seventeen years old when my relationship with Kelly ended. My dreams of romance had ended in compromise, bitterness, and regret. I walked away asking, "Is this how it has to be?" I felt discouraged, confused, and desperate for an alternative to the cycle of short-term relationships in which I found myself. "God," I cried, "I want your best for my life! Give me something better than this!"

God answered that plea, but not in the way I had expected. I thought He'd bring me the ideal girlfriend or totally remove my desire for romance. Instead, He revealed through His Word what it meant to submit my love life to His Will—something I'd never truly done. I wanted God's best but hadn't been willing to play by His rules.

Over the past four years, I've come to understand that God's lordship doesn't merely tinker with my approach to romance—it completely transforms it. God not only wants me to act differently, He wants me to think differently—to view love, purity, and singleness from His perspective, to have a new lifestyle and attitude.

"Smart Love"

The basis of this new attitude is what I call "smart love." Paul describes this kind of love in Philippians 1:9–10:

> And this is my prayer: that your love may abound more and more in knowledge and depth of insight, so that you may be able to discern what is best and may be pure and blameless until the day of Christ.

Smart love constantly grows and deepens in its practical

knowledge and insight; it opens our eyes to see God's best for our lives, enabling us to be pure and blameless in His sight.

Sentimental Gush

The Message paraphrases Philippians 1:9–10 this way: "Learn to love appropriately. You need to use your head and test your feelings so that your love is sincere and intelligent, not sentimental gush."

Have you ever been guilty of "sentimental gush," allowing your emotions to dictate the course of a dating relationship? Many people do this. Instead of acting on what they know is right, couples let their feelings carry them away

I've engaged in my share of sentimental gush. While dating, I made many decisions based on superficiality and ignorance. I could so easily say "I love you" to a girl, feigning selfless devotion, but in truth, selfishness and insincerity motivated me. I was primarily interested in what I could get, such as the popularity a girlfriend could give me or the comfort and pleasure I could gain physically or emotionally from a relationship. I didn't practice smart love. I lived "dumb love"—choosing what *felt* good for me instead of what *was* good for others and what pleased God.

To truly love someone with smart love, we need to use our heads as well as our hearts. As Paul describes it, love abounds in knowledge and insight. To "know" something is to understand or grasp it clearly and with certainty. "Insight" is an instance of understanding the true nature of something, the ability to see the motivation behind thoughts and actions.

With this definition in mind, let me ask you a few questions. Does love motivate the guy who sleeps with his girlfriend when it will scar her emotionally and damage her relationship with God? Does sincerity motivate the girl who leads a guy along then breaks up with him when she finds someone better? No! Both people exemplify selfish motivation. They need to "get smart" and realize how their actions affect others.

In recent years, I've tried to let sincere and intelligent love guide me, and as I've done this, I've come to some pretty intense conclusions for my life. I've come to realize that I have no business asking for a girl's heart and affections if I'm not ready to back up my request with a lifelong commitment. Until I can do that, I'd only be using that woman to meet *my* short-term needs, not seeking to bless *her* for the long term. Would I enjoy having a girlfriend right now? You bet! But with what I've learned as I've sought God's will for my life, I know that a relationship right now wouldn't be best for me or for the one I'd date. Instead, by avoiding romance before God tells me I'm ready for it, I can better serve girls as a friend, and I can remain free to keep my focus on the Lord.

> I have no business asking for a girl's heart and affections if I'm not ready to back up my request with a lifelong commitment.

Knowing What Is Best

Waiting until I'm ready for commitment before pursuing romance is just one example of smart love in action. When our love grows in knowledge we can more readily "discern what is best" for our lives. Don't we all desperately need that discernment?

After all, when we engage in guy-girl relationships, we face some pretty hazy issues. Don't get me wrong—I believe in absolutes. But in dating, we don't only have to make wise choices between absolute wrong and absolute right. We also have to evaluate all parts of our dating relationships to make sure we don't go too far, allowing ourselves to get pulled into something we should avoid.

Here's an example. Let's say that someone at school asks you out. How do you seek guidance about what kind of person you can go out with? Try looking up "dating" in your Bible's concordance. You won't get far. Or maybe you've gone out on a few dates with someone, and you just kissed for the first time. It was exciting. You feel as if you're in love. But is it right?

How do we find answers to these questions? This is where "smart love" comes in. God wants us to seek guidance from scriptural truth, not feeling. Smart love looks beyond personal desires and the gratification of the moment. It looks at the big picture: serving others and glorifying God.

"What about me?" you might be asking. "What about my needs?" This is the awesome part: When we make God's glory and other people's needs our priority, we position ourselves to receive God's best in our lives as well. Let me explain.

In the past I made the starting point of my relationships what I wanted instead of what God wanted. I looked out for my needs and fit others into my agenda. Did I find fulfillment? No, I only found compromise and heartache. I not only hurt others, I hurt myself, and, most seriously, I sinned against God.

But when I reversed my attitude and made my main priority in relationships pleasing God and blessing others, I found true peace and joy. Smart love unlocks God's best for our lives. When I stopped viewing girls as potential girlfriends and started treating them as sisters in Christ, I discovered the richness of true friendship. When I stopped worrying about who I was going to marry and began to trust God's timing, I uncovered the incredible potential of serving God as a single. And when I stopped flirting with temptation in one-on-one dating relationships and started pursuing righteousness, I uncovered the peace and power that come from purity. I kissed dating goodbye because I found out that God has something better in store!

Pure and Blameless

The final benefit of seeking smart love is purity and blamelessness before God. This purity goes beyond sexual purity. While physical purity is very important, God also wants us to pursue purity and blamelessness in our motives, our minds, and our emotions.

Does this mean we'll never mess up? Of course not! We can

only stand before God because of His grace and the sacrifice of His Son, Jesus. And yet this grace doesn't give us license to be lax in our pursuit of righteousness. Instead, it should urge us to desire purity and blamelessness even more.

The Story of Ben and Alyssa

Ben started dating Alyssa during his senior year in college. For quite some time, he had planned to marry the summer after he graduated. Since he and Alyssa were both deeply attracted to each other, he thought she was "the one."

In a letter, Ben told me how he had grown up with very high standards in his dating relationships. Alyssa was another story. While Ben had never so much as kissed a girl, kissing was practically a sport for her. Unfortunately, Alyssa's values won out. "When she looked at me with those big brown eyes like I was depriving her of something, I caved in," Ben wrote. Their relationship soon became almost entirely physical. They maintained their virginity but only in the technical sense of the word.

A few months later, Alyssa began to be tutored in chemistry by another Christian guy whom Ben had never met. "That was a mistake," Ben wrote angrily. "They were studying chemistry all right—body chemistry!" Alyssa broke up with Ben and the next day was hanging on the arm of her new boyfriend.

"I was crushed," Ben told me. "I had violated my own standards, and more important, God's standards, and it turned out that this wasn't the woman I was to marry." For several months Ben wrestled with guilt but finally laid it at the foot of the cross and moved on, determined not to make the same mistake twice. But what about Alyssa? Yes, God can forgive her, too. But I wonder if she ever realized she needs that forgiveness. When she passes Ben in the hall at school or sees him in the cafeteria, what goes through her mind? Does she realize she played a part in tearing down his purity? Does she feel pangs of guilt for breaking his heart? Does she even care? . . .

The Selfish Pursuit of Short-Term Romance

I believe the time has come for Christians, male and female, to own up to the mess we've left behind in our selfish pursuit of short-term romance. Dating may seem an innocent game, but as I see it, we are sinning against each other. What excuse will we have when God asks us to account for our actions and attitudes in relationships? If God sees a sparrow fall (Matthew 10:29), do you think He could possibly overlook the broken hearts and scarred emotions we cause in relationships based on selfishness?

Everyone around us may be playing the dating game. But at the end of our lives, we won't answer to everyone. We'll answer to God. No one in my youth group knew how I compromised in my relationships. I was a leader and considered a good kid. But Christ says, "There is nothing concealed that will not be disclosed, or hidden that will not be made known" (Luke 12:2).

Our actions in relationships haven't escaped God's notice. But here's the good news: The God who sees all our sin is also ready to forgive all our sins if we repent and turn from them. He calls us to a new way of life. I know God has forgiven me for the sins I've committed against him and against the girlfriends I've had. I also know He wants me to spend the rest of my life living a lifestyle of smart love. The grace he has shown motivates me to make purity and blamelessness my passion.

I'm committed to practicing smart love, and I invite you along. Let's make purity and blamelessness our priority before our all-seeing, all-knowing God.

Looking for Love in the Wrong Way

Shaniqua Sockwell

Shaniqua Sockwell was a hopeless romantic about love—until she started dating. In an attempt to feel that she was loved, she began a series of relationships with guys who said that they loved her but nevertheless treated her poorly. Like Sockwell, many teens pursue unhealthy relationships as a way to compensate for a lack of self-esteem. Sockwell advises teens to look for self-worth within themselves, not from other people.

As a child, I always saw love as a magical force that could draw two people together, and they would be that way forever. I read about love in fairy tales, saw it in movies, and heard it on the radio in songs. But I never experienced it in real life.

A Hopeless Romantic

I guess you could call me one of those hopeless romantics, because I always believed magical, undying love was possible, even though another part of me got to thinking that this love thing must be some kind of hoax. It seemed so wonderful in fiction, but never in reality. At least not for me.

Unlike a lot of girls around my block, I didn't want to get love

From "Learning to Love Again," by Shaniqua Sockwell, *Foster Care Youth United*, November/December 1995. Reprinted by permission of *Foster Care Youth United*. Copyright 1995 by Youth Communication, 224 W. 29th St., 2nd Fl., New York, NY 10001.

from all the wrong people. These girls took love wherever they could find it, mainly from men who were much older than they were, and they would endure getting pregnant and experimenting with drugs. They were so desperate for love they'd go with anyone. I was determined not to go down that road.

I would watch men and women holding hands, kissing, and looking into each other's eyes, sharing special messages that only they could understand. I would wonder, "Why can't I have that? Just for once I'd like to have someone tell me they love me and really mean it."

Like Isn't Love

After a while, I got tired of feeling like I didn't need someone in my life, so I started dating. I soon wished I hadn't.

Instead of taking things slow, I would instantly get caught up in the guy I was dating. Looking back, I realize I mistook like for love, and love for like, so it's no wonder I got hurt so many times.

Because of my parents' lack of affection, I didn't really know the difference between the two. But love is a strong word. It shouldn't be said or used unless you mean it, and Lord knows I've had my fair share of heartache from men who used this word to control me. They all knew my one weakness, that I was in great need. From that, they drew upon their ability to hurt me.

> I was looking for a loving relationship to replace [my] missing self-esteem.

One boyfriend would tell me he cared for me, and said it so sincerely that I almost believed him. But if he cared, why did he sleep with my cousin just because I wouldn't give it up?

Another boyfriend said that he liked me a lot, that I was funny and sweet, and I wasn't like most of these other girls out here. But is liking me not telling me that he made two girls pregnant and that he was also cheating on me?

The first guy I fell in love with (or rather became infatuated with) told me he loved me because he could talk to me. We discussed science fiction, art, music, and everything else. When we kissed, I saw fireworks. But is love not calling me, standing me up, and then saying "f--k you" to me all the time?

One guy who told me he loved me said I reminded him of his mother. How sweet, but is being in love with me telling my mother that you're breaking up with me before you tell me? And then making some lame excuse about only wanting to be friends, and asking me to wait for him? As if he expects me to stop dating just for him!

No Decent Men

After all this, it's no wonder that I became a cold, heartless female. Only a fool would put up with this for as long as I did. I began to dislike men with a passion. I stopped dating because I felt that I had been hurt enough and being alone was far better than being with someone who made me feel bad.

It seemed that I couldn't find a decent man, at least one who didn't want to get me "between the sheets." But on the other hand, I didn't want to believe that all men are dogs, because I know not all of them are. So what was I supposed to think about men?

I began to wonder why I was in need of love so much, why I was so dependent on having someone to call my own. That was when I realized that I never had someone in my childhood to show me any kind of affection, which is why I didn't receive or look for love the right way.

The Meaning of Love

For years, I didn't really know what the word love meant. I mean, I know what it meant, but I didn't know how to express it, give it or receive it because I didn't receive it as a child.

My biological mother always had a funny way of showing how much she loved me. The closest kind of affection I ever got from her was, "Yeah, I love your dumb a--, now go do the dishes!!" She didn't know what kind of effect this had on me, even when I did the dishes with tears coursing down my cheeks.

Actress Nia Long once said in an interview, "The first man you ever fall in love with is your father." But what if you don't know who "father" is? What if all you had was a "daddy" who did drugs and came in all hours of the night and went around with a bunch of different women who you could never imagine calling "mom"? Would you love "daddy" then? My daddy told me he loved me all the time, but, like mom, he had a funny way of showing it.

Jim Borgman. Reprinted by special permission of King Features Syndicate.

By looking at how my parents treated me as a child, I realized I had to love myself and accept myself. I've always had low self-esteem, and I felt bad because I've always been considered "different" from everyone else. (Because of how I dress, how I talk, etc.)

But I've come to see that being different is a good thing, because for one, you aren't following the crowd and two, you're being your own person and not worrying about impressing everyone else.

Basically, I was looking for a loving relationship to replace that missing self-esteem. But I had to realize that another person doesn't give you that self-esteem, you have to feel it inside yourself before you enter a serious relationship.

And although I haven't come completely full circle when it comes to how I think about myself, I can now say that I love myself a lot more than I did a few years ago.

Looking for a Fantasy

Through talking things out with people and thinking about my past relationships I discovered exactly what my problem was. I was looking for love not in the wrong places, but in the wrong way.

I was searching for my Nubian prince, my knight in shining armor. A fairy tale man. But we hopeless romantics too often forget that fairy tales should be left where they belong. This is not to say that fantasy men don't serve a purpose. They help you visualize the kind of person you want to be with, the kind of person you like.

But I was attracted to fantasy figures because I didn't have a successful male figure in my childhood. I had no idea of what kind of person I should be attracted to. Maybe I was looking for a father figure and a boyfriend at the same time.

My Needs First

Instead of looking for a fantasy, I started to put my needs first. For example, one of my exes used to stand me up on dates. I couldn't stand it, but I'd let it slide because I really liked him. But then I realized that I was ignoring my own feelings. So I looked for someone who wouldn't stand me up.

Today, I am much happier. I have a man who loves me as much as I love him. We see each other often. We write love letters. We talk. And even more importantly, he realizes that I have a working brain and that I use it.

But even though I love him, my senses are keen and aware that a relationship could end at any time. Maybe it comes from being hurt so much and developing a distrust of men. I don't want to be the one working overtime to keep the relationship going, never getting any credit, and then be left holding the pink slip.

But time has a way of healing old wounds, and I've learned to be comfortable with myself, whether I'm in a love relationship or not.

Waiting for the Right Person

Faleisha Escort

Many teens start dating before they're ready because they don't want to seem different from their friends. Faleisha Escort had several "relationship guinea pigs"— guys that she dated just to find out what dating was all about. These dating experiences made her realize what she wanted (and didn't want) in a relationship, and now she's decided to stay single until the right person comes along.

I didn't start developing romantic relationships with guys until my junior year in high school. Before then, I just saw guys as pals that I could always bug out with.

When I decided I wanted to start dating, it was mostly because my friends were experimenting with relationships and I wanted to be closer to them and participate in their discussions about their experiences with guys.

Talking to my friends made me curious. They told me things like, "When you're in a relationship, you're supposed to sacrifice for the other person," and, "You got to always keep your man in check."

I wanted to find out for myself whether their theories were correct.

Relationship Guinea Pigs

I had at least three boyfriends in high school. (I'm in my first year of college now.) I think the main reason I was attracted to these particular guys was the fact that they were easy.

Don't get me wrong, I liked them. But the main attraction was that they were easy prey!

I already knew that they liked me, so I didn't have to work that hard to get them. They were my relationship guinea pigs.

None of these relationships lasted longer than a month or so, because I wasn't as serious as I thought I was, and neither were the guys. That doesn't mean we didn't exhaust ourselves trying.

But we always ended up playing these roles I wasn't comfortable with. I was "mother," trying to guide and protect my man, while he was "father," the authority figure trying to control me.

Doing What They Wanted . . . for a While

I found out my friends were right about having to make sacrifices to be in a relationship—but I was the one doing all the sacrificing.

The guys I went out with were always saying things like, "Oh, I want to be with my friends today," or, "I want to see this movie, not that one." I was just expected to sit back and have no opinions or objections.

> I'm not going to settle for a guy who is easy to get.

I would go along for a while, doing what they wanted instead of what I wanted. If they asked me to hang out with their friends, I would, even if I didn't really want to.

But if I asked them to hang out with my friends, they would just refuse. Of course I got tired of that and ended the relationships. But I still felt disappointed and disenchanted.

It seemed like my high school boyfriends just could not get beyond "what I want" or "what I say goes."

Tekken 3 or Me?

The moment I realized I wanted a different kind of relationship came one night last summer when I was out with my (now) ex-boyfriend Derek (not his real name).

We were at the movies, killing time, waiting for the show to start. So we went downstairs to the theater's little arcade section to chill.

As soon as we got there, Derek headed toward the change machine and began popping quarters in one of the games.

At first, I'm like, "OK," since we were there and all, but then it got ridiculous. I was just standing there bored while Derek spent nearly half an hour pumping quarter after quarter into the Tekken 3 machine!

He must have gone through at least $5 worth of quarters! And get this: He has the game at home.

I knew right then and there that I was going to break up with him after the movie.

The way he was acting made me feel like I was less important to him than the video games in the arcade.

The fact that he was spending all this money (like he was Donald Trump on a spree) combined with his lack of consideration for any of my feelings was the last straw.

My Dream Guy

Since becoming a free woman again, I've been thinking about what I want from my next relationship and how to go about getting it.

For one thing, I have higher standards for myself and I am not going to take just anyone anymore. I'm not going to settle for a guy who is easy to get.

The kind of guy who would immediately spark my interest is, of course, someone who I consider cute, or at least fair, in terms of looks. Hey, looks aren't everything, but they do count!

Next comes personality and character. It's important that the guy genuinely likes and cares about the same things I do. (A guy who is cute but boring would immediately be canceled out as relationship material.)

He would be a strong believer in God. He would have had a spiritual upbringing—that's important because that's where he got his basic philosophy about life and his attitudes toward women.

He would love and respect his family and get along with them very well.

His intelligence level would be equal to mine. And his morals would give him self-respect and respect for the people he cares about.

And he would not be the type who claims to want a monogamous relationship but can't seem to stop flirting with other feminine faces. I hate that.

Friendship First

Because I think you need to know all these things about a person before getting serious, I think a successful long-term relationship is most likely to stem from a strong, committed friendship.

If you've developed love, trust and mutual respect as friends and withstood the tests of disagreements, rumors and gossip, etc., then surely you are prepared to handle the not-so-different challenges of a romantic relationship.

I believe that if I develop a meaningful, long-term friendship with a guy I find to be both mentally and physically attractive, then I'd be able to move into a relationship more comfortably than with someone I barely know.

Though I was friends with a few of the guys I went out with in high school, they weren't long-term friends. I really didn't know them like I thought I did.

Later on I would feel naive. I would say things like, "What the hell did I see in that guy!"

The Next Step

Now I will wait, browse around, explore new landscapes (slowly) and develop long, meaningful friendships with guys I am interested in before I decide to move into something more serious. After all, they may be great as pals but nothing more.

After making that transition from a long-term friendship to a romantic relationship, I think I would also feel more secure about the issue of sex (which will surely come up sooner or later).

If a guy who has stuck by me emotionally for years asked me to have sex with him, I'd be more comfortable discussing it and more likely to consider it than if a guy I barely knew asked me to have sex with him after only three weeks.

I think the good thing about a long-term relationship with the right guy is the joy and security I would find in sharing my life fully and intimately with another person. I would be able to fall in love completely.

Commitment Is a Challenge

It would also be more of a challenge for me to be with the same person for months and years and still love him enough to not get tired of him. That is the way I love my family and I would really like to experience that with a guy.

A short-term relationship allows you to step in and step out with little or no remorse. A long-term relationship, on the other hand, allows you to get so deeply involved and attached that you can't really help falling in love and truly sharing yourself.

One day, I want to be able to say, "Gee, he knows me so well," and, just as important, "Wow, I know him so well."

Do I feel like I'm ready for a long-term relationship? I don't really know, but I am intrigued.

I know it would be a challenge to wake up every day and be with the same person for so long and still be committed. But I feel that when I am ready to take that stand, I will be committed all the way.

Why You Should Only Date Your Friends

Alexander Zorach

Although some people say that dating a friend will inevitably ruin the friendship, Alexander Zorach argues that you should *only* date friends. If you are not friends with someone, he says, that can only mean two things: You don't know each other very well, or you know each other but don't want to be friends. Whatever the case, it's obvious that you shouldn't be dating a person whom you can't call a friend.

Many a time have I heard the saying: "Relationships ruin friendships." Most people will agree with that statement. You may have even seen it in action, or had it happen to you. You think about it, and it makes sense. Therefore, you make yourself a rule: "Never date a friend." You vow to hold true to this new rule . . . you make it your most important rule of dating. Wow! This is cool . . . you are going to save yourself a lot of pain now!

Does this sound like you? Unfortunately, this rule is probably the worst thing that you can do to yourself. In fact, you should be doing the exact opposite. "What are you thinking? Are you insane?" you say . . . just read on:

From "Only Date Friends?!?!?!" by Alexander Zorach, *Teen Advice Online,* at www.teenadviceonline.org/dating/datefriends.html. Reprinted with permission.

Well, let's think. What are all the possible reasons for not being friends with someone?

1. You don't know them well enough to be their friend.
2. You know them and you don't want to be their friend (for whatever reason—it doesn't matter what).

Using Common Sense

Now, let's just use a little bit of common sense here. We'll look at each case individually. If there were a person you knew, and you really did not want to be their friend (for whatever reason), would you want to be in a relationship with them? Think about it. No. You wouldn't. If there was something that kept you from being friends with someone, it would obviously be reason enough not to be into a closer relationship with them, since a relationship is closer than a friendship.

Ok, so what is the only other possibility? Well, that is that you don't know the person well enough to be their friend. Would you really want to enter a relationship with someone you didn't know well enough to know if you wanted to be their friend? No. Of course not. If you don't know them well enough to be friends with them, you *definitely* don't know them well enough to be in a closer relationship with them.

> When you really like someone, *become* their friend before you even think about anything else.

It's that simple. There is a reason that people use the phrase "more than friends." A relationship is more than a friendship. Don't become more than friends until you are friends first. Ok, so the new rule will be "Be friends first." This means that when you really like someone, *become* their friend before you even think about anything else.

The Benefits of Dating Your Friends

Let's look at the benefits of this new rule:

1. If you meet someone new, and become friends with them

first, you can get to know them on a personal level, and then decide if you really want a relationship with them. Sometimes you might really want a relationship with someone at first, and then you get to know them, and you realize that they aren't really right for you. In this case, you've avoided the pain of a failed relationship, and you've made yourself a wonderful friend in the process!

> It [is] downright absurd to try to make a relationship work without a friendship.

2. If you become friends with someone, and then build the relationship from that point, if the relationship does end, you can remain friends. Maybe that won't happen in every situation, but if you are not friends first, you can be sure that there is no way that you will be friends afterwards.

3. A friendship is built on so many of the same things that a relationship is. Those things include trust, caring, and a mental and emotional connection. In this sense, a relationship is a natural extension of a friendship. Looking at it this way, it would be downright absurd to try to make a relationship work without a friendship.

Stay Friends, Always

If there is anything more that I have to say, it's that when you do find yourself in a relationship, you should make sure to *stay friends, always.* That means *during* the relationship, and afterwards. Make sure that your boyfriend/girlfriend *is* your best friend. If you keep it that way, you will save yourself so much unnecessary pain.

Is It OK to Date More than One Person at a Time?

Dear Lucie

In the following selection, a teenage girl asks advice columnist Lucie Walters whether it's OK to date two guys at the same time. Lucie tells the teen that there is no reason why she should not date more than one person at the same time—as long as the people she's dating know where they stand. Teens who enter into exclusive dating relationships oftentimes find themselves getting too serious too soon, Lucie argues.

Lucie—The other day the boy I have liked for the longest time asked me out. And of course, I said "yes." Today, another boy I kind of like asked me out. I like my boyfriend, but I like the other guy, too. I love them both. What should I do?

—Very Confused

Very Confused—Lots of girls would envy your position, but I know it's a tough situation.

I assume the first guy's asking you to go out means you are now his official girlfriend (known as "going steady" in the olden

From "Girl Wants to 'Go Out' with Two Guys," *Adolessons* column of February 28, 2001, at www.lucie.com. Reprinted by permission of Lucie Walters.

days). If you have agreed to be this guy's girlfriend, you must honor that commitment. I don't know how old you are, or what "going out" includes.

Your situation is the perfect example of why I disagree with this current custom. Dating both of them at the same time is probably not even considered an option to you.

I mean, teens are always checking each other out and meeting new ones. Wanting to get to know or spend time with more than one person at this time is so normal and healthy.

As I understand it, teens think that if they date someone other than the person they are "going with," they are cheating. I'm talking about going on a date, not having sex.

Also, I've been told that if a teen, especially a girl, simply dates (no sex) more than one guy at a time, she gets a bad reputation.

What Is "Cheating"?

Does "cheating" mean having sex with another person or just dating another person?

I think this "serial monogamy," going with one person only until that relationship ends, then moving on to the next, is not a good or safe idea. It automatically throws the couple into a pretty intense and serious relationship. Pressures and expectations develop too fast. Also, it limits opportunities to do different things with different friends. Many times teens hardly know each other when they decide to "go with" that person.

> I think this "serial monogamy," going with one person only until that relationship ends, then moving on to the next, is not a good or safe idea.

For any custom to change, one person has to ignore or defy it, which often brings rejection from peers. But that's how change occurs. One person feels strongly enough about something to refuse the status quo.

It's your call. I'm not suggesting you are to attempt to change all this.

It's OK to do what you really want, which is to spend time with both of them. Explain that you don't want to get serious with any guy right now. Know that if you stand where you really want, they may both walk away.

Openly Gay and Dating

Jon Barrett

Gay and lesbian teenagers have long been forced to conceal their sexual orientation and keep their intimate relationships secret from family and peers. In the following selection, Jon Barrett writes that increasing numbers of gay and lesbian teens are coming out of the closet—and doing so at younger and younger ages. In the process, many are openly dating their same-sex partners, allowing them to experience this important rite of passage the same way their heterosexual peers do. Barrett is associate news editor of the *Advocate,* a national gay and lesbian magazine.

Marc Robinson, a 17-year-old from Milwaukee, didn't know how good he had it until the day he spoke to a group of gay senior citizens. "It's weird to hear how they weren't able to come out until they were, like, 50," he says. "They didn't know what it was like to be with someone. Then, when they [did finally date], they had the same type of problems teenagers have with their first relationships."

Although the stories the seniors told Robinson may have had an "I walked ten miles in three feet of snow" quality, they vividly illustrate how times have changed. That's especially true when the seniors' experiences are compared with Robinson's:

From "Going Steady," by Jon Barrett, *The Advocate*, April 10, 2001. Used by permission of Liberation Publications.

Out of the closet at 15, he's had three relationships, the longest lasting five months. "I know people who have been in relationships for, like, two years," he says. "I have two lesbian friends who are never apart. Like, if you say one of their names, you say the other. That's just how it is."

Openly Gay Dating Lives

And that's just how it is for thousands of high school students across the country. Despite the very real threats of verbal and physical abuse many of them still face, gay teens are not only coming out younger every year, they're also leading openly gay dating lives with a panache that would surprise gay people only ten years their senior.

Take 18-year-old Peter Viengkham and 18-year-old David Purtz, for example. The suburban Fort Lauderdale, Florida, couple have dated off and on for more than a year. They even occasionally spend nights together in their parents' homes. "My mom knows we're going to have sex anyhow," Viengkham says. "She's like, 'I don't want them to do it in a car because we won't allow them to do it here.'"

Or consider 17-year-old June Washington and 18-year-old Jeanette Sanders of Philadelphia. The two have been going steady ever since their first date a year and a half ago, when they went to see the film *Double Jeopardy.* "It turned out we didn't see much of the movie," Sanders says, acknowledging, almost under her breath, that she and Washington shared their first kiss in the back row of the theater that night.

"These kids are coming out and experiencing things that I should have at their age," says 32-year-old Javier Smith, who leads a gay youth group in Boise, Idaho. "A lot of times they surprise me with their maturity and the things that they've done. But other times I'm surprised at how immature they are, and I have to remind myself that they are only 16 or 17."

Aside from the Internet, gay student groups—there are more

than 800 of them registered with the Gay, Lesbian, and Straight Education Network—are the biggest reason for the upsurge in out and proud dating among teens, says Caitlin Ryan, coauthor of *Lesbian & Gay Youth: Care and Counseling*. "It was difficult ten years ago for a gay youth to meet another gay youth," Ryan says. "But these groups are providing an opportunity to have peers and to learn about being gay through your peers."

Rites of Passage

According to a survey conducted by Lisa Love, a health education specialist whose work includes gay youth issues in the Seattle school district, the two topics, besides coming out, that members of these groups want to talk about most are dating and sex. "Kids are either talking about relationships they're in, they've been in, or frustrated that they're not in," Love says. Even though many of the groups do not directly address dating issues, they bring teens together in an atmosphere in which they can at last enjoy the same rites of passage that their straight peers take for granted.

In Boise, for example, the youth group is the primary social outlet for gay teens, including 17-year-old Nick Rutley and 18-year-old Kayla Tabb. The only openly gay student at his high school, Rutley says he "would be beaten alive" if he were seen holding hands or kissing Travis Harrison, the 16-year-old he's been dating for the past few weeks. Nevertheless, he and Harrison plan to go to the prom together this spring. "I'm a little bit nervous," Rutley says. "I've talked to my parents, I've talked to the principal, and I've talked to a lot of my friends and asked them to be there, just for safety, in numbers."

Tabb started dating when she was 16 and has had two girlfriends, both of whom were 20 years old. However, she's not currently dating. "I've got too much stuff going on right now just with trying to finish high school," she says. She did recently try to date the one other girl who regularly attends the youth group, but "it was supposed to be sort of a messing-around sort of thing, and she wanted a relationship," Tabb says. "So I decided it needed to stop."

Viengkham helped establish the gay student group at his high school but met Purtz on America Online. "Everybody I know happens to meet people on AOL," he says. "I met other people [online] before David, but I guess you would call those flings," Viengkham says. "David was the first person I went out with, technically. Once we met, he actually drove up to my house. It was a really fast kind of thing, like, 'Oh, let's meet.'"

Telling Their Parents

While just meeting someone used to be the biggest dating-related obstacle for gay teens, today's youth say their dating conundrums aren't so different from the ones their straight peers face, including how to tell parents about relationships.

Washington and Sanders haven't come out to their parents about their sexual orientation or about the year and a half they've been dating. "To talk to [my mom] would be tough," Sanders says. "I mean, she sort of knows stuff and asks about it, but I never verify." The couple only came out to their friends when they realized they needed the support they weren't finding at home. "We decided we needed to tell people [about the relationship] because whenever we got into problems with each other, there was nobody to turn to," Sanders says.

Those, like Viengkham, who can talk to their parents often turn to them when the relationship gets bumpy. "My mom gives me advice and says, 'Maybe he doesn't know you're feeling that way,' or 'Maybe you should talk to him,'" Viengkham says. Others, like Tabb, say their parents try almost too hard to be accepting. "My mom will bring things home and say, 'Look, this has a rainbow on it,'" Tabb

> "Gay youth want to be in relationships for the same reasons other youth do."

says. Still, she says, it was comforting to tell her mother about her first girlfriend: "She gave me a big hug, and then she started to cry."

Sex

Where sex fits into the relationship—if at all—is another cause for concern, especially for a generation hit with images from TV shows like *Queer as Folk,* which often equates gay life with no-strings sexual encounters. But many teens seem to take a more cautious approach than the boys on Showtime. "I'm going to wait for quite some time before I even consider having sex with [Harrison]," Rutley says. "I have to know that [our relationship] isn't just casual, that there is a commitment of sorts."

Viengkham says his gay friends are more sexually active than his lesbian friends, but he doubts the difference is as much a gay-versus-lesbian thing as a male-versus-female thing. "I could go up to any straight guy or any gay guy and ask them how much sex goes through their mind, and they would answer honestly, 'All the time,'" he says.

Breakups

The hardest part of all, of course, is when a relationship ends. "Initiating relationships, especially in a small town like this, is often nothing more than 'I'm gay and you're gay,'" says Boise youth-group leader Smith. "But I sometimes spend night after night answering phone calls at ten o'clock at night from kids asking me the same question over and over again: 'Why did they break up with me?'"

Indeed, breakups are one point where gay teens diverge from their straight friends. The end of a relationship can underscore just how little gay relationships are recognized.

"Gay youth want to be in relationships for the same reasons other youth do," Ryan says. "And I think it's wonderful that there are so many opportunities for them to find each other so they can actually date in high school. But when they break up and the nature of the relationship isn't really understood by their peers or their family, I think that can be an extremely isolating and vulnerable time."

However, feelings of isolation and vulnerability are exactly what teens are supposed to be experiencing at this age. Relationships are about personal growth and experience—and sometimes the pain that goes with them. Now more than ever, gay and lesbian youths are able to learn the lessons of growing up at the same time their straight peers do. "I learned a lot in my last relationship, and I've learned a lot being single," says Harrison. "I've definitely had a lot less emotional pain being single than being in a relationship. In the end, what motivates me to be involved in another serious relationship again is [simply] the desire to love and be loved."

Point of Contention: Do Interracial Relationships Work?

As recently as the 1960s, interracial marriage was still illegal in many parts of the country. Today, this is no longer the case. Although interracial relationships are still frowned upon in some places and by some people, it is common for people of different races to date and marry. Some social critics believe that within this century, a majority of Americans will be multiracial as the result of marriages between different races.

Still, the question of interracial dating is not clear-cut, especially for teens. What follows are two contrasting viewpoints about the issue. Daniel Snow says that if two people love each other, they can overcome any hurdle—including problems that may arise because of racial differences. On the other hand, Vanessa R. says that interracial relationships are bound to fail in most instances. She maintains that most interracial couples have difficulty overcoming the conflict and misunderstandings caused by having different cultural beliefs and lifestyles.

Love Can Overcome Racial Differences

Daniel Snow

One of the most controversial topics in our society is the dating between people of different ethnic backgrounds. It is something that I felt should be addressed, as I have seen several questions to Teen Advice Online concerning this dilemma.

Love Should Overcome All Boundaries

I will keep this very brief, because I think it is very simple. Basically, I believe that love should overcome all boundaries—including racial differences. However, I think it is very important to ask some very important questions because love requires commitment. I think it's important to sit down with your potential partner and discuss this commitment very openly. Here's a

> Love should overcome all boundaries—including racial differences.

checklist to test your level of commitment to making an interracial relationship work.

- Are we both willing to sit down together and discuss this with our families, working out any concerns or problems they have with our dating each other?
- Are we both willing to be strong together to resist the social problems generated by people who lack understanding and/or display racism?
- Are we both willing to work together to overcome the odds and make a strong, solid relationship that will stand the test of time?
- Are we both willing to accept the difficulties our children would be faced with if our relationship led us to that point?

Dealing with Other People

The thing I am trying to stress is that, like any other situation, you should consider the impact upon other people. How will it impact your family? Your friends? Your future children? Don't take this decision lightly. It is likely to impact a lot of people. When you make the decision to move

58

forward, follow through with your commitment.

- Talk with your families openly and honestly.
- Recruit and establish the support of everyone close to you.
- Take the time to let your relationship grow into something simple and beautiful.
- Don't let anyone or anything steal your joy.
- Keep things simple. Be devoted to one another and committed to the relationship.

From "Interracial Dating," by Daniel Snow, *Teen Advice Online*, at www. teenadviceonline.org/dating/racial.html. Reprinted with permission.

Interracial Relationships Don't Usually Work

Vanessa R.

Interracial couples may have recently become very popular, but are they really working? Two people from two different backgrounds will likely experience a significant number of challenges and communication barriers. With different cultures come different customs. With different customs come misunderstandings. With misunderstandings come pain and grief.

> Not only can interracial relationships result in unhappiness for the individuals involved, but they can also affect family members.

Not only can interracial relationships result in unhappiness for the individuals involved, but they can also affect family members. There might exist language barriers between families, making it difficult for the couple to live harmoniously with each other's loved ones. This can cause unnecessary conflict and broken relationships.

Let's suppose an interracial relationship goes on to become an interracial marriage. The problems suddenly become more serious. Interracial couples are constantly haunted by questions such as, "Which culture will my child belong to? What cultural values will I instill in my child? Will my son or daughter be ostracized from both ethnic backgrounds because s/he is mixed? Will they be confused as to their identity and heritage?"

> Opposites might attract, but can they really survive?

What it all comes down to is what we try so hard to ignore: two people from two different cultures are not the same. They have different backgrounds, different customs, different beliefs, different ideas, and different lifestyles. Opposites might attract, but can they really survive?

From "Interracial Relationships: Two Viewpoints," by Vanessa R., *Fazeteen. com*, Summer 2000, at www.fazeteen.com/summer2000/htm. Reprinted with permission.

Chapter 2

Dating Problems

Dealing with Unrequited Love

Mike Hardcastle

"Unrequited love"—love that isn't reciprocated—can be one of life's most painful experiences, for both teens and adults. What should you do if you confess your love to someone, only to be told, "let's be friends"? Counselor Mike Hardcastle advises teens in this situation to swallow their romantic feelings and attempt a friendship. The friendship may develop into something more, but if not, he says, you still will have made a close acquaintance.

Q: I have a big crush on this guy in a grade higher than me. We don't have any classes together but we are both in band and on the school paper. I know I love him because I just can't get him off of my mind. At a party I confessed my true feelings and he told me he liked me too—as a friend. He said he just wanted us to be friends right now. I really, really want to be with him, how do I make him love me?

A: You are suffering from a killer one-sided crush, also known as "unrequited love," and there really isn't much you can do to change it into a relationship. I'll be blunt. You can not *make* somebody love you. You can't even make them like you. There are no magic spells or secret tricks that will make a person suddenly feel for you the way you feel for them. Love doesn't work like that (and thank the sweet stars above that it doesn't!). Love, when it is real and returned, is one of the most amazing feelings you will ever experience. Although it is hard to accept that this person doesn't return your feelings, it may help you to know that the pain you now feel will be erased from your heart when you find someone who *does* love you back.

Now back to the issue at hand, coping with your current crush. Since he has made his feelings for you clear, namely that he wants to be friends, you really only have one choice. You have to honor his feelings and wishes. You do however have options as to exactly *how* you handle the "friendship situation." You can swallow your feelings, move on and work on having "just a friendship" with this guy, or you can harbor your feelings and hope that the future will see your friendship turn romantic. The one thing you should do is actively take him up on his offer of friendship in spite of your deeper feelings.

> By becoming his friend you get the opportunity [to] let him see a new side of you, and you get to see a new side of him.

Take heart, all is not lost! Friendship is always a good place to start. Right now he only knows a "one dimensional" you; as your friendship progresses he will come to see your many sides. With time, his feelings may even deepen into romantic interest. You say that the two of you are not in any classes together, so it is entirely possible that his "Let's be friends!" comment is not a mere brush-off, but a bona fide offer. He may want to start as friends because he doesn't know you well enough to have any deeper feelings (a sign that he is a good guy BTW), or he may be using the "friendship line" as a brush-off (a sign that he is NOT a good guy BTW). You can't be certain which of these is true until you make a go of the friendship. Work from the premise that he really wants a friendship with you until he indicates otherwise.

By becoming his friend you get the opportunity [to] let him see a new side of you, and you get to see a new side of him. In getting closer you may even fall into a relationship. Of course, the opposite is also true. As you get to know *him* better your crush, which is built on a fantasy not a reality, may disappear and *you* may lose interest in him. There are no guarantees that your feelings will stay the same through your burgeoning friendship. There are also no guarantees that his current feelings will change into love. After you become friends you may end up exactly where you are right now, in a one-sided love affair. But at this point in time, *what have you got to lose?* At the very least you gain a closer acquaintance and at the most you'll get your man!

It Isn't Easy to Let Go

Tara M. Pfeifer

The end of a romantic relationship, especially a first relationship, can feel like the end of the world. Letting go of the relationship may seem like an impossible task. Here, Tara M. Pfeifer tells the story of how she survived a breakup with her long-term boyfriend. Pfeifer says that her female friends gave her the love and support she needed to get over a broken heart.

I never was a person to date much in high school. Other things were more important. I was active in sports, music, clubs, and academics and would like to think that I excelled at most of them. So where did the guys fit in? They fit in as some of my best friends, but never anything more. But two years ago, I entered college: a new atmosphere where no one knew who I was in high school and I could start up a fresh image. So I did. And I started dating. The second relationship I had was my longest ever. And that is why it was, and still is, hard to let it go.

How We Met

John and I met through a mutual friend a few weeks into our freshman year at college. At first I thought he was one of the oddest people I had ever met, but he was also one of the more fun people to hang out with. I would have never thought that we would end up dating, but we did. After getting to know each other throughout our first semester at school, John asked me out at my parents' anniversary party in January. I, of course, was happy to oblige.

By no means was John's and my relationship "normal." We both had very distinct personalities, and when put together, we became one odd couple. We were known as the partiers. We'd go to parties together, but never hang on each other. We'd mingle amongst everyone and find each other when it was time to go home. I'd spend nights in his room, and we would watch movies and play video games until we were both beat tired. It was all a guy and a girl like me could ask for.

Things Were Great

Time went by, and things were great. He once got me the "executive suite" at a hotel for my birthday and would send me long stem roses in the summer when we were apart. (He lives an hour away from me when we are not at school.) Unfortunately, our sophomore year of college had to start.

John met new people and slowly we grew apart. It was more fun for him to go out with his buddies and drink than it was to hang out with someone that was too "chicken" to go out to the bars. (We are underage.) I still sit here and wonder what it was that eventually broke us apart, but it happened about fifteen months after we got together. And it sucked.

Our breakup was a mutual agreement. Things just weren't working out anymore, romantically. After about a week of crying, I pulled myself together though and am living to tell about it.

What Have I Learned?

What have I learned, you ask? I've learned that your girlfriends are sometimes your greatest friends in the world. I can't begin to tell you how many times I have just needed a hug and an "everything will be all right" from someone, and my girlfriends were there to give it to me. I've learned that you *can* stay friends with an ex, although things change. John moved on to another woman nearly a week after we broke up. That hurt, and still does. A day doesn't go by that I don't think of how I could have made things better and kept John with me. But I then remember the reasons that we broke up in the first place and realize that things are better off as friends. John and I still talk every Sunday night and catch up on each other's lives. It's worth the pain that I feel when he says, "I miss you" right before he hangs up with me. It's worth it to still have him in my life. I love him, and always will.

> I . . . realized that you don't have to move on in order to let go. I've had many requests for dates since the breakup, but have not felt ready to move on.

I've Let Go

Have I moved on? No. Have I let go? Yes. I once had figured that I needed to do both of those at the same time, but then realized that you don't have to move on in order to let go. I've had many requests for dates since the breakup, but have not felt ready to move on. When I stop comparing every guy I meet to John, then it is time to move on. And I'm getting there. Slowly, but surely. Flirting is one of the greatest experiences in life, and I've missed having that "no commitment" relationship with the guys I meet.

So, what is my point? It's definitely easier to grow attracted to someone than it is to let go of them. But I don't think it is necessary to let go. I have not let go of John as a friend, and I never will. What I have let go of is the love that we once had for each other and am preparing myself to share that love with someone else.

Surviving a Breakup

Carl T. Holscher

Breaking up with a first love can cause depression and even thoughts of suicide. Carl T. Holscher was devastated when he and his girlfriend broke up. In the article that follows, he tells how he overcame his depression by talking with friends and family, finding an artistic outlet for his feelings, and doing things that made him laugh.

Looking through my memory box
Hunting for glimpses of you
Scanning hard disks for your face
Trying to recall long buried files
Searching crowds for pieces of you
Just a fragment.
A lost piece
A name
A face
I miss you. Sitting here in my endless search. For a past I
    threw away.
A part of me. Gone. Never coming back. Returning.
I can still hear your voice. Calling my name.
Daring.
Among the echoes in my head.

. . . dream
. . . or a . . .
. . . memory . . .

Carl T. Holscher, 11-23-00

From "That First Love, Breaking Up, and Depression," by Carl T. Holscher, *Teen Advice Online*, at www.teenadviceonline.org/dating/breakupdepression.html. Reprinted with permission.

The poem above inspired this story.

Everyone has that first love. That girl or guy that they are 100 percent positive that they will stay with forever and never break up and their love is unbreakable. Isn't that a wonderful feeling? It is, until you realize that one day love will end. Love is wonderful, but love also hurts. All great things come to an end, it is said, and when love ends it can really hurt. It is normal that some people get depressed and suicidal. Again, let me stress that these feeling are normal and thousands of other teens deal with them. You are not alone! I dealt with heavy depression. I could not hear the name "Kris." I would burst out into tears at any mention of her. This was even after she cheated on me. She slept with another guy while we dated. Let me tell you, it gets better with time. You have to forget the person who you broke up with. It did not work. And if it did not work the first time, it probably will not work again, so getting back together will not solve any problems. I know this will not be easy, and I am not saying that it will be. But here is how I beat my depression.

I talked to my friends and my parents. I let them know how I was feeling and they really helped.

My friends told me about how they had also lost loves. It felt good that I was not alone, and because she was my first girlfriend I did not know what was normal after a breakup.

They really helped me through getting over the initial shock. I blamed myself. I tried to figure out where I had gone wrong, what I had done.

> My friends could only do so much. I knew the rest of the battle I had to fight on my own.

Truth is, I didn't. She had cheated on me, and that told me that she did not love me. I felt used and confused. After treating this girl like a goddess for the three years I knew her and the eight months we dated, I felt very hurt.

My friends could only do so much. I knew the rest of the battle I had to fight on my own. So I did.

I sank my hurt and pain into my art. I wrote poetry, lyrics, stream-of-consciousness ramblings.

I took pictures with my camera. I redesigned my entire website. I worked on more digital artwork than ever. Anything to vent my hurt and confusion and anger! I knew that it would do no good to mope and feel sorry for myself. I had to vent my emotions and feelings! So I did.

> Do things that make you happy, or used to make you happy.

I engrossed myself in Monty Python movies that made me laugh.

Laughter and venting are the two best ways to beat depression. That is what I did. I got all of the bad feelings out onto paper or onto my computer.

These worked for me. I suggest you try them. They work if you let them.

However, DO NOT keep all the pain inside. Do not carry it around with you! You will still be hurt and just get more and more depressed, possibly suicidal. You need to release that pain.

Ways to Beat Depression

1. MOST IMPORTANT: You have to want to get better and WORK for it. If you do not want to help yourself, no one else can help you.

2. Indulge yourself. Do things that make you happy, or used to make you happy. Let your friends take you out and have a good time. Relax and focus on the good, not the bad.

3. Focus on the good!!! Do not think about how bad you feel. Think about how much fun you used to have. Do not think that life is over because someone has left you. It's not!

4. Find another girl/guy. This may seem impossible, but it will be for the best. There are six billion people on the planet, and you are lying to yourself if you think you cannot find another person to love and that will love you back.

5. Act silly! Laugh! Rent any Monty Python movie, or an-

other comedy you enjoy, and sit and just laugh! Laughing makes everyone feel better. Laugh, laugh, laugh! (Come on, you know this will make you feel better.)

6. Light! Sit in a lighted area, get outside and get some sun! Being in the dark just adds to your feelings of sadness. Get outside into the light of the sun!

7. Devote yourself to something. I used art because that is what I loved! Write, paint, sculpt, scribble, design webpages, play in Photoshop with pictures, grab a camera and take pictures, go to the mall and shop, exercise until you are exhausted, take a long walk and think, make a list of pros and cons to your situation.

8. Get help. You cannot do it all alone! It helps when you have someone there to help you along, whether this be an offline or an online friend.

Coping with a Painful Breakup

Chris

In the following article, a teen named Chris offers two steps for coping with the end of a special relationship. First, he says, you must accept that you will feel sad for a while and should express your feelings of sadness by talking with someone. Second, he advises, you must work to put your life back together by reaching out to friends and finding activities that you enjoy.

Breaking up can be no fun. Okay, sometimes it can be a relief, but usually it hurts when a special relationship ends—even if you're the one who ended it. Here's some advice on making it through the rough spots.

First, Accept Your Feelings

It's okay to feel sad. You're not made of rubber and you can't expect to instantly bounce back from a breakup. You might find it useful to write down your thoughts or make a drawing or painting. Be honest with yourself—you don't have to show it to anyone.

If you're feeling mad, don't just sit and simmer. Do something physical like going on a long bike ride or a fast run. Many people find that being out in nature helps them get a handle on their emotions. You might want to find out if there's a wooded trail or a lake you could trek around.

The time right after a breakup can be tender—maybe you've lost some dreams for the future, or maybe your ex has broken your trust. You'll have to decide for yourself how much time you want to spend with friends and how much time you'll want by yourself to think things over. Most people do find it helpful to talk about the breakup with someone they trust. Although things may seem bad now, hang with it. Breakups are almost never fatal, and things will get better with time.

You'll have to decide for yourself if you want to try being friends with your ex-boyfriend or ex-girlfriend. Some people like to try becoming friends right away, but many people find that they need to feel separated from their ex for a while before they can become friends again (if they ever do).

Second, Don't Mope Too Long

While feeling sad is part of recovering from a breakup, eventually you have to put your life back together. When you start to feel better, reach out to people and find things to do. Join some new group, call three people every day, make plans for the weekend, take up running, read a book. Your days will go by much faster if you fill them with things you like to do. You'll meet new people and you'll spend less time thinking about your old relationship.

> You can't expect to instantly bounce back from a breakup.

If you can't find an activity that suits your tastes, why not become an instigator? You could invite a group of people over for pizza and get in the habit of getting together every week, or meet with a group to play soccer every Sunday. It's a great way to get some new blood into your life.

Although breaking up is never fun, it's survivable. Remember that you're a whole person just as you are, and you don't need to be involved with someone else to be fun, likeable, or interesting.

My Boyfriend Is Controlling

Dear Lucie

In the following selection, a teenage girl tells advice columnist Lucie Walters that she is afraid to break up with her obsessively jealous boyfriend because she believes no one else would want her. Lucie encourages the girl to recognize that her boyfriend is trying to control her and advises her to seek her parents' support in breaking up with him.

---

*L*ucie—I really need help from you. I'm eighteen and have been dating this guy (eighteen) for over two years. The first year was great, but, after that, we got involved in sex. Since then, he has changed. He is treating me like his pet (can't do this, can't do that, etc.).

His jealousy is over the limit. Sometimes he can't even control his emotions. He makes me feel ashamed in front of my friends, but he's not hitting me. He has changed me into a person I don't know. I'm no longer myself.

I want to break up with him, but I just can't. I'm afraid of him. I'm also afraid of losing him, because he has been a part of my daily life. I can't face being alone without him, but I can't live with someone controlling my life. I really need to get away from

From "Girl Has Controlling Boyfriend," *Adolessons* column of September 1, 2000, at www.lucie.com. Reprinted by permission of Lucie Walters.

him, but if I do, I'm afraid no guy will want me because I'm no longer a virgin.—Needs Help

Needs Help—You are right about needing to break up with him, but wrong about no guy wanting you because you are not a virgin. Look around you, the evidence is to the contrary, so don't worry one more second about that.

I'm glad you realize you are not yourself. He may have changed some of your behaviors and beliefs, but the real you is still inside and beginning to emerge. Always remember you have the real power over yourself.

You think you would be alone, but the opposite is true. You would begin to reconnect with your family and friends. I'm sure they miss you.

Humiliation in Front of Others

One of the reasons you think you still need him is because he has conditioned you to think you can't live without him. You gave an example of one of the tried and true control techniques: humiliation in front of others.

Another technique is shaming. My guess is that he is the one who put the idea (lie) in your head that no one else will want you because you are not a virgin. That's sexual shaming.

You think he doesn't have control of his emotions, but he does. Just look at when and around whom he "gets out of control." I'm betting it's mostly when you are alone, and surely not in front of your family or other adults.

We don't know how he will react when you decide to end the relationship. If you are afraid of him, I'm sure there's good reason. Plan for a difficult time.

Getting Your Parents Involved

Tell your parents what's going on and get them involved. DO NOT try to break up with this boy when you two are alone. Have your parents as backups and within earshot. Also, break the news in your territory (your home). Your parents may need to "reinforce" your decision. Don't hesitate to contact law enforcement officials if he threatens to hurt you or members of your family.

I understand that he has been a big part of your life for over two years. You will probably miss him and feel sad for a while, but you are doing the right thing because his behavior will get worse.

Talk to your parents today. Don't hesitate to tell them because you are afraid they may find out you've had sex. Your physical safety is the issue.

Dating Violence: The Dark Side of Teen Dating

Fern Shen

In the article that follows, Fern Shen maintains that there is an alarming trend of dating violence among American teens, with at least 25 percent of teens saying they have experienced physical violence in a relationship. An increasing number of teens are engaging in abusive relationships whose dynamics resemble "battered spouse syndrome." This syndrome is characterized by a batterer who is abusive because of a need to assert power and a victim who accepts abuse due to low self-esteem. In many cases, teenage girls enter into abusive relationships as a way to obtain the attention they lack at home. The story of Lynn Ann Kenny and Garry V. Leinbach illustrates the horror of a physically violent relationship. Fern Shen is a staff writer for the *Washington Post.*

Three years ago, Anne Arundel County teenager Lynn Ann Kenny began dating a seventeen-year-old boy who, she says, regularly slapped and punched her, called her fat and once flung her across the room.

Last month, Garry V. Leinbach was found guilty in Anne Arundel County Circuit Court of assault and battery for a December 1992 beating that sent Kenny to the hospital with a smashed nose, black eyes, and bites, blood and bruises all over her body.

But asked to describe the toughest part of their three-year relationship, Kenny, of Glen Burnie, cited neither the bruises nor the insults.

"The hardest part was recognizing that he wasn't calling anymore, wasn't coming around, and that I had to start all over again," said Kenny, eighteen, who was fifteen when she started dating Leinbach.

An Alarming Trend

Guidance counselors and therapists say the relationship between Kenny and Leinbach reflects an alarming trend among teenagers in the Washington area and across the country. An increasing number are engaging in abusive dating relationships that are nearly identical to adult battered spouse syndrome, down to the victim's low self-esteem and the batterer's need to assert power, specialists say.

Many researchers consider teenage dating violence an extension of the sexual stereotyping and violence that infects U.S. society on all levels, from dysfunctional families to popular culture and corporate suites. Some see it as part of a continuum that ranges from sexually harassing jokes and comments to stalking, serious assault and rape.

Although official statistics are scarce, the handful of studies conducted in recent years by researchers in this country have found that at least twenty-five percent of teenagers say they have experienced physical violence in a dating relationship, according to Santa Monica, Calif. therapist Barrie Levy, who surveyed the literature for her 1991 book *Dating Violence: Young Women in Danger.*

In the Washington area, school consultant Deborah Simmons

surveyed more than 300 teenagers as she conducted dating violence workshops in high schools in Loudoun County and elsewhere in Northern Virginia. She found that about one-fourth of the youths said they either had battered or been battered by their dating partner.

Those familiar with more urban school systems put the numbers higher. It is difficult to measure violence among dating teenagers, guidance counselors said, because much of it takes place off school grounds when couples are alone. Police and prosecutors say they have no statistics on arrests because dating violence is not a separate crime category. The cases generally are closed to public view because, unlike Leinbach's, most are processed in juvenile court.

In the District, the D.C. Superior Court is adding a teenage counterpart to the court-ordered treatment program for adults who batter their spouses. The new program will be for thirteen- to eighteen-year-old boys.

"The need was clearly there—offenders were coming in that were younger and younger," said Desiree Dansan, acting supervisor of the D.C. court's domestic violence treatment team.

The phenomenon has led women's advocates to call for earlier intervention to prevent abusive relationships as early as junior high school.

"After twenty-five years of consciousness-raising about domestic violence, girls are somehow still believing that this behavior is an expression of love," said Leslie Wolfe, executive director of the Center for Women Policy Studies. "It means we have to do a better job, earlier, of helping girls believe in themselves. We've got to seize every teachable moment with boys."

"He Was Everything"

He was "clean" and "well-mannered" and had "preppy looks"—those were the qualities that first attracted Lynn Kenny to Garry Leinbach.

"He was everything I thought I wanted in a boyfriend," she recalled in an interview. "He did whatever I wanted—we got ice cream, went to the park, he cooked me dinner."

"He showed me the attention I wasn't getting at home," she said, noting that her extended family includes three siblings, two nephews across the street and a mechanic father and secretary mother who work long hours.

After about three months, Kenny said, she began to see another side to Leinbach, then a seventeen-year-old senior from a nearby high school. He wanted to be around her all the time, tried to isolate her from her parents and girlfriends and became wildly jealous, she said.

"The first time he pushed me," she said, "I didn't think anything of it—a lot of guys push girls." The first time he hit her, the slap "was hard enough to leave a red mark on my face, hard enough to make me cry," she said. After that first blow, she said, he cried and apologized and she forgave him. The pattern was set.

As the violence escalated, Kenny said, he hit her in the arms and face. What precipitated the blows usually was his suspicion that she was flirting with the only people he would let her be around—his friends, she said.

"Most of the time, I would look at the floor and say nothing—I just tried so hard never to give him a reason to hit me," she recalled. He distanced her from her girlfriends, she said, by telling them she had said mean things about them.

When her parents asked about the welts and bruises, Kenny said, she told them she had fallen over some furniture

> Many researchers consider teenage dating violence an extension of the sexual stereotyping and violence that infects U.S. society on all levels.

or been in a car accident. She also was sneaking out of the house at night to sleep with Leinbach in a van he would park nearby.

"I hated it, because I was always lying to my parents, and I wasn't raised like that," she said. But she was afraid to defy him.

"I was scared of him; I felt trapped."

Her parents, meanwhile, were growing increasingly upset about the relationship but felt helpless to stop it.

"Every time I confronted her about the bruises, she told me a lie," said Kenny's mother, Billie Kenny. "He showed her how to climb out the window, how to make up her bed with a baby doll sticking out of the covers so it would look like her."

Like a Brainwashing

Eventually, Billie Kenny said, she saw Leinbach slap her daughter, but she could not persuade the girl to break up with him: "It was sort of like a brainwashing. She didn't eat anything; she was on the phone with him all the time. It was like we'd lost her."

Lynn Kenny said she began dieting in response to Leinbach's growing criticism. "He was always telling me I should lose weight, that my legs were fat."

"We'd be out shopping and he'd point to some other girl and say, 'Why can't you look like that?'" said Kenny, a small person of slender build.

Kenny said she mustered the courage to break up with Leinbach after he choked her because she had talked to a former boyfriend. But then he began calling the house constantly, once phoning nine times in fifteen minutes. "I went back with him because it was the Christmas holidays and I wanted to give my family a break," she recalled. "I told myself I would just try and get through Christmas."

When Billie Kenny learned that her daughter was getting back together with Leinbach, she recalled, "I cried hysterically. I drove around for hours with my older daughter, just crying my heart out."

The final incident occurred on Christmas Eve. Kenny and Leinbach were in the parking lot of a Glen Burnie pool hall when some boys made a crude comment to Kenny. Upon hearing it, Leinbach became incensed and attacked Kenny.

The assault, which took place inside Leinbach's van, "was the most brutal beating I have ever seen, short of ones that lead to a death," said William Mulford, the Anne Arundel County assistant state's attorney who handled the case. The photographs of Kenny show big purple bruises, scratches and red bite marks all over her face, arms and back.

Mike Ritter. Reprinted by special permission of North America Syndicate.

"It seemed like an eternity that he was hitting on me. I was seeing white flashing lights. He was just screaming at me," said Kenny, who suffered a bruised kidney and smashed nose, among other injuries.

"I was saying, 'I'm sorry, I'm sorry, I'm sorry' to my parents in the hospital," she recalled, "and they said, 'You've got to start thinking of yourself!'"

She never went back to him after that. Leinbach was found guilty of one count of assault and battery in that case. He also pleaded guilty to assault and battery in another incident in which he beat and choked her. . . .

Kenny said she doesn't like to speculate on why she stayed with Leinbach for three years: "I just tell myself I learned from it."

"She Wanted to Be Hit"

Garry Leinbach's description of their relationship is quite different. Although admitting that he has a problem with his temper and sometimes resorted to physical violence, he blamed Kenny for inciting him.

"Psychological abuse can leave scars too, you know," he said.

"She knew how to press all my buttons," Leinbach, twenty, said in a telephone interview. "She wanted to be hit. Something wasn't right [to her] unless she was hit.'"

He described their relationship as a battle for control: "Some weeks, she'd be on top of the relationship, other weeks, I'd be on top."

Leinbach said that when his relationship with Kenny began, it was "just for sex," but that he soon grew to love her. "That was her power over me—that I loved her," he said.

Leinbach claimed that Kenny was "promiscuous" and that she "lied, cheated on me and stole from me." (Kenny strongly denied those accusations.) Reacting to her behavior, he said, "I might have slapped her some, but not with a closed fist."

Asked about Kenny's contention that he often hit her if he thought she was looking at other boys or men, Leinbach said she misunderstood his anger.

"I never got mad at her for looking at another guy; I got mad at her for denying looking at another guy," he said. "I would say,

'Why are you looking at him?' and she would just dead-faced lie about it."

At times, Leinbach made an effort to stress that he is taking responsibility for his actions.

"I want people to know I'm seeking help, I definitely regret it now," he said. "I'm sorry and I really apologize to the entire United States."

"I've got to learn, when I get angry, to walk out of the room," he said. "I need to get my self-esteem jacked up so if I do get into a predicament with a girl where she cheated on me, to pull away, to leave."

At other times, Leinbach seemed eager to blame Kenny. When the subject of support groups for batterers and their victims arose, Leinbach said, "A bunch of talking won't help."

What would help lessen dating violence? he was asked.

"I think girls need to be taught to be less promiscuous," he replied.

He also said that many of the bruises on Kenny's body were the result of her anemia. "She bruises easily," he said. "If I just flick her, she's going to have a bruise."

As for the Christmas Eve incident, Leinbach said he remembers little because he had had ten drinks and taken Xanax, a tranquilizer: "I haven't even seen the pictures [of Kenny's injuries]. I don't think I want to see them."

> "Girls are somehow still believing that [violent] behavior is an expression of love."

One thing he remembers from that night is Kenny hitting him in the head with her high-heeled shoe.

"I did hit him," she said, "in self-defense, to try and get him to stop."

Since the Christmas Eve assault, Leinbach said, he has been living with his father in Harford County.

Like Kenny, he said he expects it will be a long time before he attempts another steady relationship.

"It's like a battle," he said. "Women want to deem men evil, and men want to deem women evil."

A Reflection of the Culture

Researchers are at a loss to provide a definitive explanation for teenage dating violence, though many see it reflected in the sexual stereotypes that permeate American youth culture in its music, movies and videos.

"Think of this rap music, in which women are denigrated, where it's okay to be called a bitch—all of this has an impact," said Shelly Gold, a therapist with Adolescent Treatment and Family Therapy Services of Montgomery County.

Most counselors and therapists, however, place a large part of the blame on pressures teenagers feel to have a boyfriend or girlfriend.

"These girls feel like it's their job to get a boyfriend and hold on to him, and all their self-esteem is through him," said Judith Feldt, a victim advocate with the Anne Arundel County state's attorney's office. "That's why they never talk about it to anyone; that's why so little of this reaches the courts, where it belongs—they don't want to lose that boyfriend."

Though counselors occasionally encounter instances of girls hitting boys, they say the vast majority of batterers are male. Boys who batter typically exhibit insecurity, a tendency to deal with conflict through violence and the need to exert power and control, they say. In some communities, the problem is exacerbated by the culture of drugs, violence and poverty, according to counselors.

Many therapists said dating violence among teenagers and preteens often falls through the cracks of the legal system because the girls are too young to stay in battered women's shelters and too old to be aided by child protective services workers, who focus on young children victimized by members of their own households.

Maryland, Virginia and the District, like most states, do not allow an unmarried person younger than eighteen who is childless and living at home to obtain a civil protection order, the chief protection available for battered spouses. Judges issue the orders to bar alleged batterers from coming into contact with the person they are accused of beating.

> "[Abused] girls feel like it's their job to get a boyfriend and hold on to him, and all their self-esteem is through him."

"We get more and more calls these days from parents saying, 'My daughter is being abused,' and we can't do anything about it" unless the girl is willing to press charges, said Michaele Cohen, director of the YWCA Women's Center in Annapolis, which runs a battered women's shelter.

Students say they encounter the problem among their peers frequently.

"I know a girl whose boyfriend hit her in the head with a golf club," said Gracy Reihl, seventeen, of Glen Burnie High School, at a recent workshop for teenagers who counsel their peers.

"She was over at his house. They were going to go to the beach, and he said, 'You can't wear that bathing suit,' and then he hit her in the head. Another time he pushed her down the stairs."

"I said, 'You've got to get help.' She told me, 'If a guy really loves you, he hits you to let you know how much he loves you,'" Reihl recalled. "I just don't get it. She comes from a real well-to-do family, she's real pretty, every guy in the school would love to go out with her."

A Largely Ignored Problem

Until recently, victim advocates say, school officials largely ignored the problem, in part because they feared it would require frank discussions of sex and violence that might offend conservative parents.

"But the guidance counselors are being faced with it more and more, and they don't know how to handle it; they're begging for help," said Joan Braden, a therapist for Montgomery County's Abused Persons Program who conducted a workshop on the subject for county teachers and counselors.

Schools vary widely in their recognition of the problem. A few states, such as Minnesota, have made dating violence prevention a mandatory part of the system wide curriculum. In Virginia, some teachers include sessions on dating violence in the elective Family Life Education courses.

Gradually, school officials and others are perceiving the special tragedy of abusive relationships among the very young, said Janice Thomas, a school guidance counselor who has been helping Lynn Kenny.

"It's one thing to have adult women who stay with a batterer because they're married, or have kids and are economically dependent," Thomas said. "But it's so depressing to me to hear young girls who already think they're trapped."

Chapter 3

Dating and Sex

Why I'm a Virgin

Tara Bonaparte

Whether you're a girl or a guy, teenage virgins have to put up with a lot of flack from their friends. Tara Bonaparte, who is a virgin and proud of it, tells teens that it's important not to be swayed by other people's opinions about sex. Tara advises teens to wait until they're ready to have sex—and to be aware of the potential consequences of sex, such as sexually transmitted diseases and pregnancy.

Wuz up, people!!!! Well, this is the high yellow, big mouth, funny writer who comes correct with all the facts, coming at ya with an article that is strictly for the ladies. (But guys, feel free to read too.)

This article may help you understand some of the stresses that we ladies have to go through in being virgins. And ladies, this article may help you to understand things about yourselves.

This article can also speak to male virgins. The same way that some females have to worry about males, males also need to worry about some females. Because there are a lot of girls (and you girls know who you are) who want to take away the virginity from the last batch of virgin males that exists.

When my mother and father were growing up, it was a good thing for a girl to be a virgin. My grandparents made sure that all of their five daughters (including my mom) ran around claiming what was between their legs was 14-carat gold. My grandparents always let their daughters know the importance of being a virgin. And that is why I know the importance of being a virgin.

No Respect

Today it seems as if nobody has any respect for themselves. Girls (not all of them) are running around having sex with any and every boy who says they love them.

And the boys. I just have no words. They are running around reproducing more children than rabbits. Having sex with any girl who has a big butt and a nice smile.

Where did the respect for being a virgin go?

Being a teenager, I know that one of the biggest things that teens worry about is self-image. We teenagers are always worried about what our friends think. We're always trying to be down with the latest craze.

And when I look around, the newest craze is for people to talk about all the sex they have. And if you happen to be that one teenager who hasn't experienced the "wonder" of having sex, it can be very difficult.

Name Calling

"Man, you ain't had sex yet?"

"You scared or something?"

"What, are you gay?"

If you are a virgin, these statements are probably very familiar to you. Most of the time they come from your friends, but sometimes they even come from your partner. These statements can make the strongest person feel like an idiot.

Well, let me shine some light on these problems.

Lying About Sex

If you've heard these comments from a friend, then there are some things that you really need to know. Ninety-nine percent of the time your friend is lying about her own sex experience. And liars always try to make themselves look good by putting others down.

Teenage Pregnancy

- The pregnancy rate among sexually experienced teenagers dropped from 254 to 207 per 1,000 (19%) in the last two decades.
- 85% of teenage pregnancies are unplanned, accounting for about one-fourth of all accidental pregnancies each year.
- Six in ten teenage pregnancies occur among 18- to 19-year-olds.
- Among sexually experienced teenagers, about 9% of 14-year-olds, 18% of 15- to 17-year-olds, and 22% of 18- to 19-year-olds become pregnant each year.
- Only 25% of the men involved in the pregnancies among women under age 18 are estimated to have been that young.
- Teenage pregnancy rates in the United States are twice as high as in England and Wales, France, and Canada; and 9 times as high as in the Netherlands and Japan.

Alan Guttmacher Institute, 1994.

Does your friend usually bring up the topic of sex when he/she is around a large group of people? If your friend does, then I'm sorry to say that he/she is probably still a virgin too. Because if a person is having sex, there is no need to brag about it.

If you've heard those statements from your partner, there is only one reason he/she is telling you that. He/she is obviously trying to make you feel bad that you're a virgin. Bad enough to give it up to him/her.

Don't be fooled, because if your partner really loved you, then he/she wouldn't be trying to make you rush into a serious, life or death decision. And believe me, it is.

To all the virgins out there—if your mama or daddy didn't tell you this, then I think that it is time that we have "The Talk." So to everyone who is reading this article, take these words as seriously as the air that you are breathing.

To me, being a virgin is the most precious thing in the universe. And when I finally do decide to lose my virginity, it will be when I'm ready. And when I'm in love.

Don't let anyone pressure you into doing anything that you don't want to do. And please don't be fooled by those silly lines like "I have needs" or "It will make our relationship grow stronger."

Give me a break. Everyone makes sex seem like a holiday in the Bahamas, but nobody bothers to explain the consequences. And there are plenty.

Party's Over

Sex (if done right) can be a beautiful thing. But everything is not beautiful about sex. So, to that young virgin who is about to take that first step to sex—listen up. I don't care where you are either. You could be at your boyfriend's/girlfriend's buck naked and just happen to pick up this article. You better get your clothes and run.

Just like they say that weed is a gateway drug, sex can lead to a baby or a serious disease. And virgins can get pregnant the very first time they have sex.

There was this one girl I knew when I was younger. Her name was Taisha. She was pretty, smart and funny. Everyone wanted to be just like her. Every time my family and I played house, I would be her. She was 18 and still a virgin. I was seven and still believed in the stork. But still, I always told everyone that Taisha was my best friend.

> Being a virgin is the most precious thing in the universe.

When I reached 12, I knew all I needed to know about sex. I knew that I could get pregnant. I also knew about AIDS. I guess

Taisha didn't know. The last I heard she was 25, had AIDS and was pregnant for her third time. And I heard that her children have the AIDS virus. Not everyone can pass on the AIDS virus to their children, and I was hoping that she didn't pass it on to hers. But she did. Sad, isn't it?

Her First Time

Taisha's cousin told me that the first person she had sex with gave her the AIDS virus. So don't sit there and say, "It can't happen to me." Because as long as there are teenagers and sex out there, it can happen to you.

> The longer you wait, the more you will appreciate sex when you finally have it.

You could be having sex for 50 years (even though the thought is very scary) and never catch a disease. Or you can have sex just once and end up with the AIDS virus. So be careful.

Along with babies and diseases, sex also gives you a reputation. And once you gain a reputation, it is going to stick with you for a long time. You could have the reputation of a "goodie two shoes," but all it takes is for you to have sex with one not-so-special person to be labeled a h-. And I know that isn't right, but unfortunately that is the world that we are living in today.

To be honest, a boy is not really going to be called anything but "The man" for having sex. So ladies, you and your boyfriend can have sex, but only you will get the bad reputation. Hmmm, something to think about.

Making Love

Now, at this point, I know you are probably saying, "Damn, this girl is trying to keep our legs closed forever."

Well, that is not completely true. I'm just trying to make sure that before anyone goes out and does something as serious as sex, they should know about the good and the bad.

There are a lot of good things about making love. But don't be in such a rush to find out what's so good. Because the longer you wait, the more you will appreciate sex when you finally have it. And you will appreciate it more if it's with somebody you really love. So people, let me end this article with a little advice.

Make your decision right, because it could change the rest of your life.

Sex Doesn't Make You a Man

Damon Washington

Teenage guys face a lot of pressure to "prove their man-hood" by having sex. In the following article, Damon Washington, a seventeen-year-old virgin, says he's glad he withstood the pressure and stayed a virgin. Even though he has been tempted to have sex, he says, he knows that deep down he wants to save sex for after he's married. To teens considering having sex, he says that sex doesn't make a guy a man, and it doesn't make a relationship closer.

I'm seventeen years old and proud to be a virgin.

I choose not to have sex because I'm still young and have a lot of life ahead of me. I have college to look forward to and having sex won't help me further my education.

Of course, the idea of having sex does cross my mind every now and then, but I already have too much to deal with in my life as it is. I have goals. I want to get married, become a writer and, if I'm lucky, to play football in the pros someday. Having sex will not make these things happen.

Until a couple of years ago I lived in the Cypress Hills Projects in East New York. I experienced everything there—guns, drugs, violence. . . . But a lot of the time the main issue was sex.

From "Sex Doesn't Make You a Man," by Damon Washington, *New Youth Connections*, September/October 1996. Reprinted by permission of *New Youth Connections*. Copyright 1996 by Youth Communication, 224 W. 29th St., 2nd Fl., New York, NY 10001.

Outside on the benches my friends always talked about how they were going to get with this girl and that girl. They would call girls "b--ches" and "h-es" whenever they wouldn't give them the time of day. In fact, I've never seen these guys do anything nice for a girl. To them, all they were were sex objects.

"What's the Matter with You?"

My friends would question me constantly about whether I ever "got any."

"No," I'd tell them.

"What's the matter with you?" my friend Kevin asked one time. "You too busy or something?"

"Yeah," I told him. "Because, unlike you guys, I want to treat girls with respect before I even think about moving to the next level."

"Man, you don't know what you missing."

My friends teased me so much that it got to the point where I almost felt I had to have sex just to get them off my back about it. But no matter how many times they asked me they still got the same answer: "I'm still a virgin and proud of it." As long as I'm happy with myself and what I have accomplished in life I don't have to prove anything to anybody but myself.

Two years ago I was in a relationship with a girl named Lynnette. We spent time together, talked on the phone a lot, showed our affection towards one another by hugging and kissing. One day Lynnette and I were talking and I asked her if she had ever had sex. She said she hadn't. Then she asked me the same question and I told her I hadn't either.

Just Being with Her Was Enough

Lynnette told me that in her past relationships sex was all her boyfriends thought about, 24-7. And when she found out that was all they were with her for she dumped them. She said she hoped that I wasn't that type of guy because if I was she would dump me too. I told her I wasn't and that being with her was all I ever needed.

We used to joke around about sex in terms of who would last the longest and how far we would probably go, but our relationship was based on having fun together. Lynnette said she wanted to be married before she had sex and I respected her for that. Not too many people our age realize that waiting to have sex can also be a good experience.

It's not that I didn't think about it sometimes, however, or that we didn't have plenty of opportunities. Once Lynnette and I went over to my house after church and my mother went out and left us all alone. We were talking, kissing and playing around, acting silly. Then we went to my mother's room to watch a movie. I was still playing around with her but Lynnette seemed more interested in the movie than me and I felt kind of neglected.

A Close Encounter

After the movie was over we went downstairs to the kitchen. Lynnette was cooking ribs and watching a basketball game on TV. She was a big time Chicago Bulls fan but I wasn't into it. I tried to take Lynnette's mind off the game by kissing her.

"Stop," she said and kind of pushed me off.

When my mother came home and we took Lynnette home I didn't say much to her because she had been ignoring me.

"What's the matter with you?" she asked. "Why aren't you talking to me?"

"Nothing," I said.

I walked her to the door and just when I was getting ready to leave she said, "Hold up. You ain't gonna give me a kiss?" I walked over, kissed her and went back to my mother's car.

Later that night Lynnette called to find out what the problem was. "Why didn't you want to kiss me when you dropped me off?" she asked.

"Because I didn't like the way you was ignoring me," I said.

"It wasn't like I was ignoring you the whole time. It's just that you kept kissing on me," she said.

"I have a confession to make," I said. "The reason I kept kissing on you was because I was kind of anxious to take our relationship further, and by us being in the situation we was in, the moment was there, anything could've happened. I was wrong and I'm sorry."

"I forgive you," Lynnette replied. "But it wasn't like I was gonna let you take advantage of me. You should know me better than that."

"I know I should've never thought about you in that kind of way," I said. "I just thought that if we continued to get to know each other like we did, then maybe something could have happened between us."

"I'm still a virgin and proud of it."

"Maybe I will have sex some day but only with my future husband on our honeymoon," she said.

It felt good being honest with Lynnette that day. It showed me that we can overcome any obstacle as long as we are honest with one another.

A Long-Distance Relationship

About six months after we started going out, Lynnette moved to Georgia, but we are still together. We have a lot of love and history to make up for, but eventually when we are reunited we will just pick up where we left off and see where we go from there. The time to have sex will come in the distant future. Hopefully we will be married and make love on our honeymoon.

Sex doesn't make a relationship—it's the love and dignity of how you feel about one another that does. I loved Lynnette with all my heart. I was faithful to her. I was there for her through the good and bad times. I was there to console her when she was sick. She once said to me that when I was with her I filled her heart up with so much joy and that is why she wants me to be hers forever. This may not seem like much to some, but to me it's what a real relationship is all about.

Call me old-fashioned, but I want to sleep with and wake up next to my future wife. To me sex is best when you've made a commitment to one person and shown how much you love and care for her.

Sex Doesn't "Just Happen"

I went out and did some interviews about how sex affects a relationship, and when I asked teenagers how they first decided to start having sex, many said the same thing: "We didn't decide. It just happened."

But sex doesn't just happen. People like me choose not to have sex and have reasons to back up our choice. Whether they want to admit it or not, the it-just-happened people allow it to happen.

It isn't fair to blame it on the other person either. It takes two to tango. "No" means "no" and if your boyfriend or girlfriend can't respect that, then you don't need to be with him or her, plain and simple.

So if you do decide to have sex, do it because *you* choose to—not to fit in with the crowd or because your partner wants you to. Do it for yourself and make sure to use protection all the time. No matter how you feel about it, sex isn't something worth losing your life over.

If, like me, you decide not to let it happen, remember, you have nothing to be embarrassed about. Virgins are winners in their own right. And when you feel that you are ready to have sex, whenever that time comes, hopefully you will make your first time a time to remember. In the meantime, there is nothing wrong with waiting for the right person to come along.

I know that making love to someone can be a beautiful thing, but I only want to experience it with someone who is going to be in my life forever.

Don't Let Guys Talk You into Having Sex

Mary O'Donnell

Maybe a guy buys a girl an expensive dinner or does something nice for her—does that mean the girl owes him sex? No way, says Mary O'Donnell. No matter what, sex is not a form of payment. Under no circumstances should a girl have sex because she feels pressured or obligated. Mary tells teenage girls not to be taken in by the lines that some guys use to try to convince girls to have sex.

There are some very simple but important rules to follow before you engage in sex. First, make sure you really know your partner; don't have sex when you don't know who you're dealing with. Just because he/she is cute or popular or tells you what you want to hear is not a good enough reason to engage in sex. Make yourself understand that you are special and someone has to prove that they are worthy to be with you—physically as well as mentally.

Guys Will Say Anything

Don't listen to the lines! Guys will try anything to get in your pants. These are just a few lines a guy might say to get you to have sex (don't fall for them):

From "Don't Listen to the Lines," by Mary O'Donnell, *Foster Care Youth United*, May/June 1998. Reprinted by permission of *Foster Care Youth United*. Copyright 1998 by Youth Communication, 224 W. 29th St., 2nd Fl., New York, NY 10001.

1. If you really liked me, you'd do it.
2. Come on, if you don't like it, I'll stop.
3. No one has to know.
4. I love you.
5. I'll give you anything you want.
6. I'll be with you forever.

Always remember when you say, "No," it means "No"! Just because he may be your boyfriend, doesn't mean you have to sleep with him. Just because your date bought you dinner, doesn't mean you have to sleep with him. Just because you flirt, doesn't mean you have to have sex. No matter what anybody says, your body is your body. You shouldn't have sex just because he thinks you owe him something. Sex isn't a form of payment for a favor someone has done for you.

The Dangers of Sex

Teen pregnancy is a growing problem. There are a lot of things you can use to prevent pregnancy—and even diseases. Think about it—you're young and if you're reading this you're probably in either a foster home or a group home. If you're in a place such as this, you're not able to take full care of yourself, so how can you take care of a child? Your baby would be given to foster care or you and your child would be placed in a mother and child facility.

> Sex isn't a form of payment for a favor someone has done for you.

There are also many diseases out there. You can catch many diseases from sex, oral sex, and even kissing. Make sure you know your partner and even if you think you know your partner, always use protection.

She Called Me a Tease When I Said "No"

Joshua

One night, Joshua brought home a girl he met at a party—but then decided that he really didn't feel comfortable having sex with her. The girl responded by calling him a "tease." Joshua said that the experience made him empathize with girls who are told that they're "asking for it" if they wear attractive clothing or act flirtatiously.

Guys talk about getting laid as often as possible. As guys, we're supposed to be gettin' it whenever and wherever we can. The hype is completely different for girls—only "sluts" give it up, right?

And if we're getting busy with a girl, and we don't get what we want, she's a "tease." I've probably said it myself a couple of times. I think it's because when you're in the heat of the moment, your blood is pumpin', and your heart is racing—to be told it's not going to happen is like missing the lottery by one number.

"No" Is Not a Joke

But I don't think this is an excuse anymore. I've been on both sides, and saying "No" comes from somewhere deep inside. It's not a joke, and it's not meant to be offensive. For a boy or girl, there will be times when having sex just doesn't feel right. Making the decision to stop isn't so much being a tease as it is respecting yourself and backing up what you feel.

I wasn't born this deep. My whole attitude on sex and expectations changed a couple of years ago when I told a woman "No" and was branded a tease.

Cruising

A new club had opened up in town and it was the hottest place to be and be seen. I went with a bunch of friends, but I wasn't there to cruise. I had just broken up with my girlfriend two weeks before, and when you're with one girl for a year, it's hard to go out and be with someone new right away. I was just looking forward to dancing and partying with my friends. And that's what I did.

Near the end of the night, my friend Linda ran into one of her old friends, Claudia. She was *fine*. We were introduced, and I could tell she was into me. She turned me on. Not just physically—she pushed that button and I became charming, smooth, flirty. When the club closed, she asked me if I needed a ride home. I already had one, and should've taken it, but I went with her anyway.

> It took me a while to stand up for what I really wanted. But it was still the right thing to say no.

If there was one moment when I was misleading or wrong, this was it. In the back of my mind I was still trippin' off my ex. But how do you say no? I wasn't taught to say no, and I'm sure my friends wouldn't have understood. So I went with the moment and the rush of having this girl dig me.

Teasing

When we got to my place she came inside. We had that nervous conversation you have when your mouths are saying words and your minds are thinking sex. But all the time my mind was also racing with thoughts about how this shouldn't be happening. I'm not into her . . . I'm not over my girlfriend yet. I really wanted to just slow it all down and relax, but we started kissing anyway and fell onto my couch.

And then I kinda just stop.

I tell her we're not going to have sex.

I try to get up and she slides her hands down my butt. She laughs and says, "Sure we are. You're not wearing any underwear." I froze.

I had forgotten about that. And it wasn't a big deal to me. I like not wearing underwear, it's kind of like walking around with a sexy secret. But when you're with somebody, this kind of secret is seen as a come-on. She assumed my not wearing any underwear meant that I left the house to find some chick and end the night without needing underwear anyway.

Not "Asking" for It

When I didn't say anything, she got pissed, called me a tease and stormed out. I wasn't laughing; I got pissed too. What does my underwear have to do with having or not having sex? I'm not sending out any messages through my briefs. I realized for the first time what a woman might feel if she's wearing a really short skirt or tight blouse. Now I see it's probably not an invitation to sex; she's got her own reasons for wearing what she wears. She's definitely not "asking" for it from anybody—so get over it.

Yeah, I admit I was confused that night, and maybe that makes me a tease. I admit that I misled her when I got into her car and let her come up to my apartment. Yes it took me a while to stand up for what I really wanted. But it was still the right thing to say no. That doesn't have anything to do with being naked beneath my jeans.

Now I listen real close when I hear a guy talk about how some girl is a tease. He probably wasn't gettin' any and has no clue why. Putting someone down is a sad way to deal with not getting what you want. She would have seemed much cooler in my mind if she'd respected where I was.

In the end I told the truth, kept my dignity, and realized that she wasn't the sort of woman I want to be involved with. If that makes me a tease, then being a tease isn't so bad.

The Unexpected Pitfalls of Losing My Virginity

Shauna

Television, movies, and books often give teens the impression that losing their virginity will be a magical experience. In the article that follows, Shauna describes her romantic vision of sex as "The Big Lie." Even though she was in love with her boyfriend and felt ready for sex, Shauna says losing her virginity was awkward, confusing, and physically painful. Moreover, she was unprepared for how emotionally lost she would feel afterward.

I didn't lose my virginity—I know exactly where I left it.

It was three days past my eighteenth birthday with my boyfriend, Curtis, who was also a virgin. We were in love—in crazy, desperate, earthshaking love, and we wanted our first time to be special.

Everything was perfect: He was a wonderful, caring, decent man. I knew I didn't have to worry about him running back to his buddies to brag about his "score." We were in my own bed, we used protection, we were "old enough," and we were relaxed and happy.

I remember the romantic way I had envisioned it happening—

it would feel wonderful and I was supposed to feel wonderful afterwards—mature and fulfilled.

"The Big Lie"

I now refer to that idea as "The Big Lie."

I'm not saying it can't be that way, I'm just saying that soap operas and romance novels don't exactly paint an accurate picture of losing your virginity.

Here's the truth:

It's awkward.

It's confusing.

It can hurt.

And for most women, having an orgasm is very unlikely.

I Felt Emotionally Lost

Worse yet, I was completely unprepared for how emotionally lost I would feel afterward.

Instead of feeling like I'd crossed some sacred threshold into true womanhood, I felt like I'd just slammed the door on ever being a little girl again. I was eighteen—an adult by legal standards—and yet there was still a little girl inside of me who wasn't quite ready to let go of who she was. I felt as if I'd given away a part of me that I could never get back.

> I was completely unprepared for how emotionally lost I would feel afterward.

I think I assumed too much. I thought that since my partner loved me a great deal and we'd given the event so much forethought, I would be left with a rosy "afterglow" instead of the emptiness I felt.

Simply because I was eighteen—older and more emotionally mature than many are when they lose their virginity—I was strong enough and resilient enough to get through it. My partner and I already had a strong relationship, so I talked to him about the feelings I was having. We worked through them together and had a loving relationship for two more years before we finally went our separate ways.

Glad That I Waited

I don't think it would have been any easier for me if I'd waited longer, but I'm grateful that I waited as long as I did—and that I chose the right boy. It helped me to deal with the unexpected feelings that came up.

Although I think we'd all like sex to be spontaneous, I've learned that it requires a great deal of thought and planning—for adults and teens alike. And that involves several things: choosing a partner, making sure you have and use protection against pregnancy and infection, keeping realistic expectations of the experience, and waiting until you know that you can handle the feelings that may come up afterward.

In the end, I have no regrets about how or with whom it happened. But I always feel so sad for the girl or boy who has their first sexual experience too early and may be unable to cope with feelings that might have been much easier to handle later on.

Why I Hate Sex

Lenny Jones

Like many teens, Lenny Jones began to feel curious about sex because of the stories his friends told about their exploits. Finally, he decided to "jump on the bandwagon" and have sex. Although he'd thought that sex would totally transform his life, after doing it he simply felt disappointed. Also, he became petrified with fear over the risk of catching a sexually transmitted disease. Lenny says that he hates sex because it only fulfills his physical needs and leaves him emotionally empty.

B efore I begin, let me tell you a little about myself and this column.

The Lenny Jones Show is my very own forum where I get to be as sarcastic as I wanna be while I "bleep," moan and groan about whatever I want, like nicotine fiends, getting my own hell hole of an apartment and, you guessed it, relationships.

Today, I'll be talking about sex. (It ain't all it's cracked up to be!)

Maybe I'm the only one who feels this way; but I have good reason to. I can honestly say that I am the king of reckless relationships.

When I was younger, relationships didn't really matter that much.

From "Why I Hate Sex," by Lenny Jones, *New Youth Connections*, November 1997. Reprinted by permission of *New Youth Connections*. Copyright 1997 by Youth Communication, 224 W. 29th St., 2nd Fl., New York, NY 10001.

If I found a girl attractive, I'd write her a little note or some-thing. If she rejected me, who cared, I'd just go home and watch cartoons or play in the park with my friends.

As I got older, the pressure started to build up to have a girl. All my friends did and it wasn't as fun hanging out with them and their girls. I felt like excess baggage.

I Felt Like a Tag-Along

When I made plans to go out to the movies with a friend and he'd invite his girlfriend, I'd feel like a tag-along. Whenever I tried to talk to him, he would be so preoccupied with her that if I walked away, he wouldn't even know I was gone.

So I went hunting and found myself a girlfriend.

Our relationship was one of those cute puppy love things. We were inseparable—wherever you saw one, you saw the other.

We were always kissing and hugging each other, talking about whatever was on our minds, and just having fun making each other happy.

We would set a time when we would both ask our teachers if we could go to the bathroom and we would meet by the stairs. Then we would run down the halls together and cause trouble. (What do you expect? We were only about 11 or 12 at the time.)

We would write little love poems and notes, then stick them into each other's lockers.

I Was Still a Virgin

I found the joy that all my friends were raving about. It actually made me want to go to school the next day so I could start it all over again.

But later on down the line, my friends started having sex. They would tell me every intimate detail—every day!

I was still a virgin and felt pretty left out again (even though whenever my friends asked if I did it yet, I would lie my "bleep" off. I would say, "Yeah, I lost it!" and deflect the attention back to them by asking why it took them so long to lose it).

But one time I got caught out there when a friend asked me if I was still a virgin, and I said no.

I Decided to Jump on the Bandwagon

He kept asking me questions about things I didn't know about and couldn't answer, so I ended up getting busted.

After that, I decided to jump on the bandwagon and have sex.

I thought sex would totally transform me.

People told me that it would "make your voice go deep," "put hair on your chest," "clear up acne," "make you more mature" and "make you be a man."

I started to feel betrayed by everyone who hyped up sex. It was like an evil cycle they just had to pass down to me.

But at the same time, I was petrified of sex. People would tell me horror stories about it.

Like one time, a friend told me that his friend had a one night stand and ended up getting a sexually transmitted disease (STD). That didn't really scare me because I was used to hearing about this in school.

But what did scare me was the STD treatment that they gave him. (They put a tube where no tube should go and would make a guy cross his legs just thinking of it.) That scared the bejeezus out of me.

Then there was my fear of HIV/AIDS.

I kept thinking about all the bad things that could happen, like condom breakage and pregnancy. (Another Lenny?—now that's scary!)

My First Experience

But I did it anyway.

Unfortunately, my first experience was nothing worth raving about.

I mean it wasn't really something that I, myself, wanted. I was curious. But mainly I was taken in by all the hype and I wanted to be down.

I had so many things to worry about, though, that after I'd had sex for the first time, I was just left sitting there thinking to myself, "That's it? I want a refund!"

And I was so petrified afterward that something might have gone wrong that I went for the most painful full check up at The Door the next day.

(Well, maybe I'm exaggerating. The physical itself wasn't painful. It was just the Q-tip test, which they gave me twice!)

I Was a Nut!

They also gave me a whole bunch of stuff to make sex safer, like rubber gloves, KY jelly, flavored dental dams, some foamy stuff and lots of condoms.

Even after that, I was still paranoid.

I was taking HIV tests every month for about four months. I was also thinking about becoming a monk or celibate and taking medication to lower or stop my sperm production. I was a nut!

After a while, I started to feel betrayed by everyone who hyped up sex. It was like an evil cycle they just had to pass down to me. They lost their virginity, regretted it, and then made it seem like the greatest thing on earth so they could share their misery.

I Still Haven't Found Ms. Right

I say that because for me, losing my virginity was like that ad for Lay's potato chips: "Bet you can't eat just one." Sex just became a weird craving, both physically and emotionally.

I craved it physically because of all that biological crap that goes on in a man's body. (I don't think I need to get that explicit.)

I craved it emotionally (and still do) because I wanted to experience love with someone I really cared about and felt an emotional bond with.

Even though I lost my virginity six years ago, I still haven't found that "Ms. Right," only "Ms. OK" or "Ms. One Night Stand."

I really want more than just the physical side of sex. I want to experience the emotional side, too. I want to find the "right" person (if there is such a thing).

I Want More

Without that emotional bond, sex still feels the same way it felt the first time—boring! If you don't give a damn about the person you are doing it with, you're missing the whole point and you're just wasting your time!

That's mainly why I hate sex. I can never put my mind to rest, only my hormones! And it leaves me an emotional wreck because it makes me yearn for the right person even more.

He Used Me for Sex

Rebecca Lanning

In the following selection, Rebecca Lanning introduces the story of "Brittany." Sixteen-year-old Brittany recalls she had moved to a new school and was feeling extremely lonely. Then she met a guy who started paying a lot of attention to her. In an effort to keep his attention, she had sex with him. She was devastated when she realized that the guy wanted nothing more to do with her. Brittany says that experience helped her learn that she needed to find self-esteem inside herself and not look for validation from others. Lanning encourages teens who are thinking of having sex to take time to think about the possible negative consequences. Lanning is a writer for *Teen* magazine.

If you didn't know her, you might think 16-year-old Brittany* had it all together. She's really cute, in a Sandra Bullock kind of way, with swingy brown hair and a smile that can light up a room. You'd think she'd never had one moment of self-doubt. But she keeps a secret tucked inside of her, a secret of shame, sadness and loss. Here is her story:

This is really hard for me to talk about. Whenever I think back on all that's happened, I feel these waves of grief. Like someone

*Names and identifying details have been changed.

Excerpted from "He Only Wanted Me for Sex," by Rebecca Lanning, *Teen,* August 1995. Reprinted with permission from *Teen* magazine.

died or something. And I want to go back and try to fix it, change the whole story so that it has a different ending, a happy ending. But I can't do that. I used to pray that I'd wake up and be my old self again. But then I'd run into him somewhere. Or someone would mention his name. Or I'd just see a car like his, and I'd fall apart.

Sometimes, my eyes would tear up and I could squeeze them shut and swallow hard and kind of swallow the pain and be OK. But other times, I couldn't shut it off that easily. Like one day at school. I was sitting there in biology, and I saw him pass by in the hall. I saw him for, what, a millisecond? And I lost it. I had to be excused. I went to the girls' bathroom and closed myself up in a stall and leaned against the door and just cried. Total sobbing. Those giant, heaving sobs, like when you can't even catch your breath. I felt so stupid, but I couldn't get a grip. And then my face was all red and splotchy, and I looked like I'd been beaten up or something. And I guess I had been, in a way, beaten up from the inside. It's hard to make that kind of hurt go away. It's not like I even want to be with him again. I mean, I did for a while, but now I just want to put it all behind me. I want it all to be like an-

> I wanted to be accepted . . . and so I gave in.

cient history. Or not even history. I want it to be like it never happened at all. I wish I could just take a giant eraser, and erase the whole thing from my life.

Trying to Connect

I think things started to unravel when my family moved. We built this house that was a mile from our old house, and we moved at the end of my freshman year. When I was a freshman, I was really popular. I was on student council, and I was a junior varsity cheerleader and I had a great boyfriend named Hayes. He was really good to me. Even though he wanted us to have sex, he never pressured me. And at that time, having sex was like the last thing on my mind. I never even considered it.

Then, during that summer, before my sophomore year, the school districts got changed, and that fall, I had to go to a different high school where I knew only about two people. Even though I tried to make friends and get involved in stuff at my new school, it just didn't come that easily for me. It was like everybody was already in their set groups. I couldn't find a niche, you know, where I felt accepted. I ate lunch by myself a lot. I was really lonely. I went to some club meetings, but nobody would really talk to me that much. I felt like I was invisible. I'd try to get together with some friends from my old school, but it's like I didn't really fit in with them anymore either. And I guess I didn't want them to know what a hard time I was having at my new school, so I didn't really reach out to them. Then Hayes and I started having problems because we couldn't see each other that much. And when we were together, I was always so bummed out that he didn't really know how to handle it. So we broke up the last week in September. And over the next couple of weeks, I sort of gave up on myself, on my chances of being popular. And then in October, I met Tad.

The Highlight of My Day

I had never felt that kind of attraction before in my life! He had wavy brown hair and brown, sort-of-flirty eyes and these shoulders that went on for miles. He played soccer, so he was really in shape. I could just look at him and melt. He had Spanish right before I did, and I always passed him coming out of the room where the class was. At first, we just smiled at each other. And then one day he said, "hi," and then pretty soon we were meeting there between classes and talking. It was the highlight of my day. Every morning when I woke up, I thought about when I would see Tad and that gave me energy, you know, to get up and get going. All morning, I'd think about stuff I could say to him. And then after we'd talked, I'd feel pumped up and that would help me get through the rest of the day.

One day when we were talking, he invited me to eat lunch with him. I thought it was just going to be us, but he showed up with two of his friends, Ward and Peter. They were juniors like him; they were on the soccer team too, and we walked over to this deli. They were pretty wild, you know, kind of loud and acting crazy. I remember, Tad pulled me on his lap. I was kind of nervous, but at the same time I was so happy, almost delirious. It felt so good just to be close to him and be eating lunch with other people. I was like a sponge. I was just soaking up the attention. I ended up paying for everybody's lunch. After that, I ate lunch with Tad, Ward and Peter every day. I wouldn't say much. But I'd smile a lot and laugh at their jokes. Sometimes, they'd ask me personal stuff, like what size bra I wore and did it hook in the front or the back. Or they'd ask me how far I'd gone with a boy. When I look back on it, I realize that these guys didn't know how to act around girls. But at the time, I thought they were really experienced. They were older. They were cute. I guess I thought I was privileged, you know, to hang out with them.

Crossing the Line

Things started moving really fast. Tad started calling me up late at night. We'd try to speak Spanish to each other. He'd sing me these James Taylor songs. He'd ask me questions about Hayes, like if he was a good kisser. And then he'd tell me about this girl named Vallie that he used to go with. I'd met her at school. She was really pretty. Tad told me about how they had had sex. He said how fun it was, but that Vallie just couldn't let herself go. She was too uptight.

One night, I went out with Tad and Peter and Ward. We just rode around and went to a couple of parties and then we ate at this pancake place. Later, after they dropped me off, Tad threw rocks at my bedroom window, and then he climbed up the gutter, onto the roof and into my room. My parents weren't there;

they were at the symphony, but I didn't tell Tad that. We talked real quietly, and then he turned off the light and stood real close to me. I let him kiss me and unbutton the top of my nightgown.

Then he tried to get me to unhook his belt buckle, but I wouldn't. I wanted to in a way, but I was scared. He begged me to let him lie down on the bed next to me, but I wouldn't do that either. He said I wasn't any fun, and I remembered what he'd said about Vallie being uptight. I wanted him to think I was fun so that he'd want to be with me.

> It's so weird how something like sex, which is supposed to bring two people closer, can actually drive a wedge between them.

The next weekend, I went out with Tad and his friends again. This time, they got some beer and we went out to this field near the airport. We all got out and were lying on the hood of Ward's jeep, watching the planes come in for a landing right over our heads. The sky would be pitch dark, and then you'd hear this roar and see this huge jet all lit up right over your head, like it was so close you could reach out and touch it. It was unreal.

The next thing I knew, Tad had grabbed a sleeping bag and he was leading me by the hand away from the jeep and into the woods. He was being sort of funny about it, sort of dancing with me. He had a couple of beers tucked in the sleeping bag, and he was trying to get me to drink one, but I wouldn't. Then he spread the blanket out on some pine straw in a clearing, and he pulled me down next to him. He started telling me how beautiful I was, how much he liked me. He started kissing me. Then he took his coat off, and he took mine off too. He kept kissing me and undressing me, and I don't know why, but I let him. I figured I could stop things if they got too intense. But the next thing I knew, he was on top of me. He was saying all these wonderful things to me, like how right it was for us to be together. He was being really gentle, really sweet. It felt so good to be close to him, but at that point I still wasn't going to give in. But then he said I was beautiful. And that made me feel so happy. I started feeling my old confidence coming back, and it's so ironic because that's when I started giving in. It's hard to explain, but I think I felt that having sex with Tad was going to make everything better. I'd just been doubting myself so much, and here was this guy who didn't have any doubts about me. It's like, he really wanted me, and in my twisted way of thinking, I sort of confused his feeling good about me with me feeling good about myself. Does that make sense? I think I wanted to be accepted so bad, I wanted to feel like I belonged somewhere again, and so I gave in.

Holding On

The next few days were kind of weird because it's like this incredibly huge thing had happened to me and yet nothing else had changed. Those crappy feelings hadn't gone away. If anything, I felt worse. I couldn't make sense of it all. Tad was still nice to me and stuff, but it's like something had shifted between us. He didn't look at me the same way anymore. Maybe it was my imagination, but it seemed like he didn't look at me at all. He looked sort of past me or through me, like I wasn't there.

At the same time, my interest in him grew even stronger. Even though I was beginning to make some girlfriends at school, I started feeling really dependent on Tad. I saw him talking to Vallie once, in front of her locker, and I thought I was going to die. He had his arm around her waist, and he was kind of tickling her, and I felt like a million knives were stabbing me all over. I was mad, but I felt like I didn't have a right to be mad. Tad hadn't promised me anything. I'd just assumed that we'd be together because we'd had sex. But obviously, he didn't feel the same way. I felt so used, so worthless. Like a piece of trash. I couldn't believe that Tad could've said all those things to me and then tossed me aside. Was all that just a big act so he could get me to have sex with him? Or had he really liked me, and then I blew it by letting him get too close?

I think maybe he was surprised that I had given in to him, even though that's what he wanted. I think maybe he liked the challenge of trying to get me to have sex more than he liked actually having sex. And I guess I wasn't much of a challenge anyway, so he sort of lost interest. Two of my new friends, Mollie and Dana, told me to forget about him. They said he wasn't worth what I was putting myself through, but I couldn't let go.

I Went Crazy

I became really clingy, calling him up all the time and crying if he couldn't meet me somewhere or see me. I constantly tried to figure out where he was. One night I was driving around with Mollie and Dana, and I saw his car parked in front of Vallie's house. I went crazy imagining that he was up in her room, saying to her what he'd said to me. Telling her how beautiful she was. Making her feel the way he'd made me feel. I was crying so bad I could hardly see the road to drive. Another time, I showed up at this party where he was. This stupid Janet Jackson song was playing, and I got right up in his face and started dancing real suggestively, hanging all over him, singing real loud in his ear. I'm sure everybody thought I'd lost it, but I didn't care. I was trying to win him back, get him to look at me the way he used to. I know I was going about it all wrong. I should've just acted like he didn't mean anything to me, but I couldn't do that. I didn't know how.

We ended up having sex again, twice. Both times I was the one who initiated it. One time was at Peter's house after school. The other time was at my house, in my room. I really regret that time especially because whenever I look at my bed that's what I think about. That will never go away. It's so weird how something like sex, which is supposed to bring two people closer, can actually drive a wedge between them.

I thought having sex would make my life better, but it didn't.

Things went from bad to worse because at least when I was a virgin I had that. But after I lost my virginity, well, I guess I felt like I didn't have anything else to offer Tad or anybody because I'd already given away the most precious thing that I had.

Looking Back

Mollie was the one who finally talked me into going to a school counselor after Christmas break. That's when I knew things were just out of control. I'd ended up sleeping with this other guy, Marty, from my old school on New Year's Eve. It's like I didn't want Tad to be the only guy I'd slept with; I didn't want him to be so special, and so I got together with Marty. That's how warped I was. But the counselor helped me sort of put together the pieces of what had happened. She helped me deal with all the guilt and stuff that I was feeling. It's been over a year now, and things are better. I can actually have a conversation with Tad and not break down. I don't even blame him so much for what happened anymore. I do think he took advantage of me. He smooth-talked me into doing something I wasn't ready for. I was at a very vulnerable place, and I was looking to him to make it all better, but he couldn't. He took something from me that I'll never be able to get back. But he also taught me something. That being self-assured, feeling good about who I am, has to come from the inside. Nobody can make me feel secure but me.

> Feeling good about who I am . . . has to come from the inside.

I'm on the gymnastics team at school now, and I was elected to the homecoming court and the National Honor Society. That meant a lot to me, but I'm still not completely over what happened. I have a hard time dating guys because I think that they know I'm not a virgin and that's why they're with me. I mean, I still sometimes feel like I'm the scum of the earth. There's this little voice inside of me that's like my cheerleader. She keeps trying to convince me that I'm OK. That I'm still a good person. But when I look in the mirror it's not always her voice I hear. Sometimes it's a nagging, critical voice.

I wish I could go back in time and change stuff that's happened. I'd give anything if I could just go back to the first day at my new school. I'd really try harder to make friends and not expect to fit in overnight. I'd reach out more. I think I'd be more honest about how hard all the changes were for me instead of pretending that everything was OK.

I'd like to go back to that night in the woods with the planes going overhead. I wouldn't have gone anywhere near that sleeping bag. No. What I'd really like to do is to go back to that first night I let Tad come in my room. I wouldn't have let things go so far.

Lessons from Brittany's Story

If you're thinking about becoming sexually active . . . sex doesn't always bring two people closer. And if you're looking for sex to help you to feel an emotional closeness with someone, you may be disappointed. Rather than creating emotional intimacy, sex can destroy it—especially if you have sex with someone before you're ready. Many teens report feelings of anger, loss and sadness after engaging in sexual activity. They may feel hurt, cold or diminished in some way. A painful early experience can take years to recover from and influence your feelings about sex for the rest of your life. Becoming sexually active is a personal decision, and it's important that you choose your first sexual experience carefully. "There's no such thing as a sexual emergency," stresses Jackson Rainer, Ph.D., a psychologist at the Brookwood Center for Psychotherapy in Atlanta. If you're thinking about having sex, you should take your time and make sure that you're prepared to handle the possible consequences of becoming sexually active. These consequences include experiencing a sense of loss or shame, as well as becoming pregnant or contracting HIV or some other sexually transmitted disease.

If you've already had sex and you wish you hadn't . . . though you might want to put the whole thing behind you and move on, it's important to examine exactly what happened and why. Did you have sex to try to get—or hang on to—a relationship? Did you do it because you felt everyone else was? Did you think it would be your ticket to cool? Or did someone pressure you?

While you can't undo what happened, you can explore the impact of a negative sexual experience and, in the process, shake off some of the pain associated with it. Once you recognize your motivation for having sex, you can better see what your values are and how you may have compromised them. Then you can begin to rebuild your moral code or your ideas about what you're willing and not willing to do. "Rather than give yourself a hard time," suggests Dr. Rainer, "look for the meaning in what happened." By exploring your role in the situation, you're less likely to repeat the activity that made you feel bad about yourself, and you can begin to look for new, healthier ways to get what you need.

I'm Glad I Waited

Laura

Although Laura wanted to have sex, she decided to wait until she was a legal adult until she did so. She says she was glad she waited. Although her experience wasn't positive in all respects, it was better than the experiences of her friends who'd started having sex at age fifteen or sixteen.

When I was a kid, I decided that I wouldn't have sex until after high school. From the vantage point of age nine, that seemed about right—an age I could imagine being but not *too* soon.

And as it happened, I "lost my virginity" a week before I left for college. It had as much to do with chance as it did with conscious planning, but I do think that waiting—whatever the reason—was a good thing for me.

Not Doing It

I started dating my first "serious" boyfriend when I was seventeen. Both of us were virgins, but we quickly progressed through the usual stuff. For months, we toed the line of "technical virginity," doing everything but actual intercourse.

Not that I didn't want to. I suppose it was the classic nice boy's myth about Nice Girls: He couldn't imagine that I would say "Yes." And I found it almost impossible to say what I

Reprinted from "Waiting Until Eighteen," by Laura, *Teenwire.com,* 1998. Copyright © 1998 by PPFA. Reprinted with permission from Planned Parenthood® Federation of America, Inc. All rights reserved.

wanted. I remember opening my mouth, willing the words to come out, and hearing nothing.

So maybe we weren't ready. (If you can't even say what you want, that's a pretty big clue.)

Eventually we broke up. (He turned out to harbor unrequited love for—I kid you not—the prom queen, who wanted nothing to do with him.) I cried a lot, then I graduated anyway, and went off to work as a counselor at a local summer camp.

And for the first time in my life I was propositioned, by three different guys. Not that I wanted to sleep with any of them (too old, too clueless, too sleazy). Even so, that summer made me realize I had a choice, that I could be attractive to someone, that I would most likely have sex at least once before I died.

Then Doing It

Then I came home and went to a party. There was a tearful reunion with my ex and . . . well, it just happened.

The funny thing was, it wasn't that big a deal—the act itself. It was pretty much what we'd been doing for the last year, plus intercourse. (Yes, we did use protection.) What *was* a big deal was *choosing* to do it—deciding I was ready, and taking the opportunity. I even went into the bathroom afterwards and stared at myself in the mirror. I didn't look different, but I did think, "You'll remember this."

> Compared to friends who had sex at fifteen or sixteen, I had a much better experience.

And I do remember—the fear, the decisiveness, the stupid song that was playing the whole time. I also remember being sort of disappointed. (I didn't even come close to the earth-shattering orgasm that was supposed to cap the event.) Looking back, I think we were both so nervous that the pleasure part got pushed aside.

So why did I wait? It was mostly luck and timing, but I like to think there was some shred of wisdom from way back—that my nine-year-old self knew what was best all along.

I'm glad I waited. The truth wasn't as simple as I might have thought when I was nine, but compared to friends who had sex at fifteen or sixteen, I had a much better experience. I felt like an equal participant—I wasn't simply trading sex for love. It was all jumbled up together, with my desire as big a part as his.

We broke up a year later. While we no longer have much in common, we do share an odd bond, and it makes us gentle toward each other. Maybe next time we meet, for dinner or coffee, I'll ask him if he remembers.

The Sex Readiness Checklist

Heather Corinna

How do you tell if you're ready for sex? Heather Corinna offers a "sex readiness checklist" as a way for teens to determine whether or not they are truly prepared for the risks of sexual activity. First of all, she says, it is important for teens to ask themselves why they want to have sex, who they are doing it for, and what they expect from sex. Next, she suggests, teens must consider the material, physical, relationship, and emotional necessities of being sexually active. Corinna is the founder and editor of Scarleteen.com, an online sexuality resource for teens.

O ne of the biggest misnomers about sexuality in our culture is that vaginal intercourse is "going all the way," and is some sort of final goal to sexuality, which is unfortunate . . . and untrue. This idea has contributed to a whole lot of confusion and disappointment for many who have first intercourse, and wonder where the fireworks and trumpets were, or why it wasn't all they thought it would be.

Sexuality has many, many different forms and facets, and we can explore it in a number of ways all of our lives. Penis-to-vagina intercourse is only one. But if you're considering having intercourse for the first time, there are a lot of things you and your partner need to know and evaluate, especially if you're coming into it thinking it is the culmination or finale of your sexuality. This checklist is applicable for just about any form of sexual activity, especially those in which there is a risk of pregnancy. Take stock, and get real!

Reality Check

Intercourse will not necessarily do any of the following for you:

- Guarantee a longer or closer relationship
- Give you an orgasm, or mind-blowing pleasure
- Feel great the first time, or feel like hell in a handbasket, either
- Give you status with your friends
- Make you more mature, or grown-up, or a "real" man or woman

There is a lot to think about when deciding if it is right for you and your partner to have vaginal intercourse for the first time. Here are a few basic questions to ask yourself, and to ask your partner.

Why Do I Want to Do This?

If either of you wants to do it because you feel you must or should, or because one of you is pressuring the other, or you're getting pressure from friends, or if you're having troubles in your relationship and you think sex will fix it, stop right there; wake up and smell the double-latte. You're completely off-base. Another thing to give you pause might be if you're fantasizing about sex based on movies or television: remember how in Tom and Jerry cartoons, Tom could hit a wall and walk away from it just fine, and you knew that wouldn't work in real life? Same goes with a lot of sex in movies and television; it isn't often as it appears. Also, if you simply want to unburden yourself of your virginity with no one in particular, you might want to think again. In most studies, nearly any woman who has handled it that way felt terrible later.

On the other hand, if you've been with your partner a while and have a solid level of other sexual experience (including kissing, petting, masturbation, and oral or manual sex), you feel you can trust yourself and your partner with limits, and you're looking to explore your sexual relationship responsibly and sensitively and for some greater intimacy, with no notion it is guaranteed and a firm grip on reality, read on.

Who Do I Want to Do This For?

If it's for you and your partner as well as you, then okay. But if it is for someone else primarily, and not for yourself, stop now. They have hands and fingers. They know how to use them to get off, and you can rest assured they've been using them long before you came along. Sex with someone else shouldn't be about self-gratification; that's what masturbation is for. If your friends are saying you should, with no understanding of your relationship, or your own needs, they're being crappy friends. Nine times out of ten, a lot of friends who pressure their friends to have sex do so because they don't feel all that good about their own choices, and want to hide behind endorsing sex to make themselves feel better. Tell them to carry their own baggage, not try and pass it off on you.

> Intercourse isn't a miracle cure for anything, and it isn't a fireworks show.

What Do I Expect from Intercourse?

It's smart to take stock of what your expectations are, and hold them against the real situation. Talk to a friend who has had intercourse who is really honest with you (or an older sibling or family member) about what you expect, and listen to their own experiences. Do a reality check. The truth is, if you have a list as long as Santa's of expectations, it isn't very likely they'll be met. Often, the less we expect, the more we often receive. Intercourse isn't a miracle cure for anything, and it isn't a fireworks show: it can be a wonderful, natural affirmation of intimacy and an excellent physical and emotional experience as long as you're ready for it and take it at face value, without romanticizing it or imagining it to be something it is not.

Am I Really Prepared to Handle All Aspects of Intercourse?

There's a lot to handle; probably more than you think. Here are what we see as the basics for what you need materially, physically, emotionally and in your relationship for your first time to be enjoyable, safe, physically gratifying, and emotionally sound. Make a checklist for yourself that includes these items, and check them as they are true.

The Big Checklist: Material Items

- I have several up-to-date, good quality latex condoms, and both I and my partner know how to use them.
- I have a large bottle of latex-safe, water-soluble lubricant (KY Jelly, Astroglide, Wet, etc.).
- I have a secondary method of birth control for use with condoms.
- I have a towel and a stock of menstrual pads.
- I have a list of local clinic or gynecologist phone numbers.
- I have a savings account I can use myself at any time (preferably with a pad of $500), and I have a "sex budget" of about $50 per month to take care of birth control, safer sex items and annual testing and sexual health care.
- I am covered under a health insurance policy, which can cover pregnancy, neonatal care, gynecological visits, sexually transmitted disease (STD) testing and/or birth control, or I have the funds to pay for these services.

Being Ill-Prepared and Unrealistic

Bear in mind the following: a good thirty percent of people never have sex again with the partner they lose their virginity to. Only about twenty-five percent of women usually report enjoying first intercourse physically (though many more enjoy it on an emotional level), and less than eight percent report orgasm from first intercourse. Those bummers most likely had to do with being ill-prepared in general, simply not knowing the basics, and overall, with unrealistic expectations.

Heather Corinna, "Ready . . . or Not?" Scarleteen.com. Available at www.scarleteen.com/sexuality/readiness.html.

The last three items are what you will need to deal with potential disease, illness, infections or pregnancy, just for starters. There is no sex, save masturbation—no matter how long you and your partner have known each other, or what you have convinced yourself of—that does not carry some risks, no matter how safe you play it. If you haven't checked all the items in that list, take care of that first.

Physical Items:

- I have had regular doctor checkups, disease and infection testing, and am in good health, and my partner has had regular doctor checkups, disease and infection testing, and is in good health.
- I understand my own anatomy and my partner's anatomy, as well as the basics of vaginal intercourse, STDs, sexually transmitted infections (STIs) and human reproduction.
- I can tell when I am sexually aroused, and also know when I am not, what I need to be aroused, or when I simply cannot get aroused.
- I can relax during sexual practices without fear, anxiety or shame.
- I can handle a mild level of physical pain.

Relationship Items:

- I am able to create limits (to say no when I want to) and can trust my partner to respect them at all times.
- I can assess what I want for myself and separate it from what my partner, friends or family want.
- I am able to trust my partner, and am trustworthy myself.
- I can tell my partner easily what I want sexually and emotionally, and when I do and do not like something.
- I can talk to my partner about sex comfortably, and be honest and forthright, and they can do the same with me.
- I care about my partner's health, emotions and general well-being, and act accordingly.

Emotional Items:

- I don't have any strong religious, cultural or family beliefs or convictions that sex for me, right now, is wrong.
- I can take full responsibility for my own emotions, expectations and actions.
- I can handle being disappointed, confused or upset.
- I have a member of my family I can talk to about sex, and friends I can go to for emotional support.
- I can separate sex from love, and do not seek to have sex to use it to manipulate myself, my partner or anyone else.
- I understand that having intercourse could change my relationship for good or for the worse, and feel I can handle whatever may happen.
- I feel I can emotionally handle a possible pregnancy, disease or infection or rejection from my partner.

One of the items on the list that gets a lot of balking is having a family member you can talk to. However, bear in mind that if you are a minor, your parent is still legally responsible for you. That means that in the event of any serious health or medical problems, legal issues or even when you visit a clinic, they have full rights to all information, and to choices made on your behalf. Take a minute to honestly think of the very big secrets you've been able to hide from your parents all your life—there aren't very many, are there? You can rest assured, you most likely won't be able to keep your sex life a secret, and to treat your family fairly, you shouldn't. They care about you, and in caring back for them you owe them the honesty required so that they can do their best for you. It may be hard at first, but I can promise you it'll be much less hard than if you surprise them with an STD, pregnancy or other problem out of nowhere.

Some things were not included. For instance, I didn't say you needed to be able to insist on using a condom if your partner didn't want to use one, because a partner who doesn't want to take good care of both of you isn't one you should be sleeping with. It's really that simple. Toss the checklist to your partner too: talk about the items on it. You may find that simply discussing the reality of the situation makes a big difference for both of you. A lot of sex is innate and intuitive, and it is perfectly normal to feel driven by our libido and our emotions, but it isn't okay to ignore good sense and responsible behavior because of those feelings and desires.

> You most likely won't be able to keep your sex life a secret [from your family], and to treat your family fairly, you shouldn't.

That's a lot to look at isn't it? Here's the deal: there isn't a statute of limitations on your sex life, and it doesn't begin or end with intercourse. You can initiate any level of it at any time during your life, and change what you want to do as you go along, determining at any time what is best for you, and for your partner(s). If you haven't checked almost all of the things on those lists, take a look at the ones you didn't check and try and figure out what you need to do for yourself right now. There is no reason to set yourself up for a fall or rush into something that won't be enjoyable or rewarding when it isn't going to go away if you wait. Be honest with yourself, and above all else, do what is right for YOU.

No Excuse for Unprotected Sex

Colleen Lee

With all of the choices of products for birth control and protection from sexually transmitted diseases on the market, says Colleen Lee, there is absolutely no excuse for teens to have unprotected sex. Lee describes the most effective common forms of protection and explains their benefits and disadvantages. Lee writes for Teen Advice Online, a website that offers peer advice to teens.

So, you've decided to take the plunge. . . . You are physically, mentally and emotionally ready to take one of the biggest steps of your life. But questions swarm through your head. What kind of protection should I use? Where can I get it? How much will it cost? I hope this article will help you choose the form of birth control and sexually transmitted disease (STD) protection right for you. These are a few of the most common and effective forms for teenagers.

Abstinence: This is your best bet to avoid STDs and pregnancy. It is 100 percent effective and is free. Abstinence involves refraining from sexual intercourse.

Cervical Cap: This is a small rubber cap filled with spermicide. The cap is then placed into the woman's cervix before intercourse. The cervical cap is about 80 percent effective against pregnancy and offers no protection against STDs. A woman must visit her gynecologist and get an exam as well as get the cap fitted before she can begin use. Insurance will often cover the cost of the cap and the doctor's visit.

Condoms: Condoms can be made with latex, plastic or other natural membranes. The most common and effective material for condoms is latex. Their job is to prevent body fluids from mixing during intercourse. Condoms are very effective against both STDs and pregnancy. When used consistently and correctly, they offer about a 97 percent protection against pregnancy. For added protection, also use spermicide. You can obtain condoms at any local drugstore or gas station. You can also obtain free condoms through a family planning clinic or order free condoms off the Internet. Many college campuses also sell condoms at very reduced rates.

Female Condom: Reality female condoms are made with a thin plastic called polyurethane. The condom is placed inside the woman's vagina. It is a long polyurethane tube with two flexible rings at the ends to help hold the condom in place. It is about 94 percent effective against pregnancy when used properly. It also helps protect against sexually transmitted diseases. Unfortunately, it can be very difficult to insert correctly, which greatly decreases its effectiveness. Reality female condoms are sold at many drugstores and cost about $2–3 per condom.

Depo-Provera: Depo-Provera is an injection. It contains a hormone similar to progesterone. It stops the woman from releasing an egg to be fertilized. The woman must receive the injection every three months in order for it to be effective against pregnancy. It offers over 99 percent protection against pregnancy but offers *no* protection against STDs. You must go to a gynecologist or a family planning clinic to receive the injection.

Diaphragm: The diaphragm is a small rubber disk a woman places into her vagina to cover her cervix. It is similar to the cervical cap. The diaphragm blocks semen from entering the uterus and fertilizing an egg. The diaphragm must be used with spermicide. They are about 80 percent effective against pregnancy and offer no protection against STDs. The diaphragm is also difficult to insert. You must visit a gynecologist to get a diaphragm fitted. Be sure to ask the proper way to insert, remove and maintain the diaphragm. Insurance oftentimes covers the cost of the diaphragm and the doctor's visit.

Teenagers and Sexually Transmitted Diseases (STDs)

- About 1 in 4 sexually experienced teenagers (3 million) acquires an STD every year.
- Infectious syphilis rates more than doubled among teenagers since the mid-1980s.
- Teenagers have higher rates of gonorrhea than sexually active men and women aged 20–44.
- In a single act of unprotected sex with an infected partner, a teenage woman has a 1% risk of acquiring HIV, a 30% risk of getting genital herpes, and a 50% chance of contracting gonorrhea.

Alan Guttmacher Institute, 1994.

Norplant: Norplant implants are six small rods inserted in the upper inside of the woman's arm. Once Norplant is inserted, it slowly releases small amounts of progesterone into the body. Norplant is 98 percent effective against pregnancy, but offers no help against STDs. The Norplant remains in your arm for several years, so you must have long-term plans to remain childless. You can get implants from a specialized clinician. Only a few places will insert *and* remove Norplant, so do your research carefully. Norplant can cost several hundred dollars.

The Pill: The pill is a combination of hormones that prevent pregnancy by stopping ovulation and by thinning the lining of the uterus. If the pill is taken very regularly (the same time every single day) it can be over 99 percent effective against pregnancy. Unfortunately, this offers no protection against sexually transmitted diseases. Using the pill in combination a second form of birth control can provide almost infallible protection. The pill also has many added benefits for women. It can lighten menstrual flow, lessen cramps, reduce risk of ovarian cancer and ovarian cysts, and improve skin condition. You can get birth control pills though your gynecologist or a family planning clinic. Some family doctors will also write a prescription for the pill. Many family planning clinics will give very reduced rates on the pill, and some clinics offer it for free for those under eighteen years of age.

The Morning After Pill: This is *not* a form of birth control and is only to be used in time of emergency. It is very helpful if you are a victim of rape or your birth control has failed (broken condom, etc.). ECPs (emergency contraceptive pills) are two large doses of ordinary birth controls. They must be taken within 72 hours after unprotected sex. ECPs are not as effective as other forms of birth control and are known to cause side effects, such as violent nausea and vomiting. ECPs can only be obtained through a doctor's visit or a visit to a family planning clinic. These pills offer no protection against STDs

I hope this gave you some of the information you're looking for. Doctor's offices and family planning clinics are always available to answer any questions you may have; don't hesitate to call them. As you can see, there are many convenient and economical forms of protection, so there is just no excuse for having unprotected sex. Keep in mind, the rhythm method and withdrawal are both very ineffective methods for teenagers, so do not rely on them to prevent pregnancy. Good luck with all the beauty and responsibilities that accompany sexual activity.

Organizations and Websites

The editors have compiled the following list of organizations concerned with the issues debated in this book. The descriptions are derived from materials provided by the organizations. All have publications or information available for interested readers. The list was compiled on the date of publication of the present volume; the information provided here may change. Be aware that many organizations take several weeks or longer to respond to inquiries, so allow as much time as possible.

Advocates for Youth

1025 Vermont Ave. NW, Ste. 200, Washington, DC 20005
(202) 347-5700 • fax: (202) 347-2263
e-mail: info@advocatesforyouth.org
website: www.advocatesforyouth.org

Advocates for Youth is the only national organization focusing solely on pregnancy and HIV prevention among young people. It provides information, education, and advocacy to youth-serving agencies and professionals, policy makers, and the media. Among the organization's numerous publications are the brochures *Advice from Teens on Buying Condoms* and *Spread the Word—Not the Virus* and the pamphlet *How to Prevent Date Rape: Teen Tips.*

Alan Guttmacher Institute

120 Wall St., New York, NY 10005
(212) 248-1111 • fax: (212) 248-1951
e-mail: info@agi-usa.org • website: www.agi-usa.org

The institute works to protect and expand the reproductive choices of all women and men. It strives to ensure that people have access to the information and services they need to exercise their rights and responsibilities concerning sexual activity, reproduction, and family planning. Among the institute's publications are the books *Teenage Pregnancy in Industrialized Countries* and *Today's Adolescents, Tomorrow's Parents: A Portrait of the Americas* and the report "Sex and America's Teenagers."

American Civil Liberties Union (ACLU)
125 Broad St., 18th Fl., New York, NY 10004
(212) 549-2500 • fax: (212) 549-2646
website: www.aclu.org

The ACLU is a national organization that works to defend Americans' civil rights as guaranteed by the U.S. Constitution. It supports confidential reproductive health care for teens and civil rights for homosexuals. ACLU publications include the monthly *Civil Liberties Alert,* the quarterly newsletter *Civil Liberties,* the briefing paper "Reproductive Freedom: The Rights of Minors," as well as handbooks and pamphlets.

Child Trends, Inc. (CT)
4301 Connecticut Ave. NW, Ste. 100, Washington, DC 20008
(202) 362-5580 • fax: (202) 362-5533
e-mail: swilliams@childtrends.org
website: www.childtrends.org

CT works to provide accurate statistical and research information regarding children and their families in the United States and to educate the American public on the ways existing social trends, such as the increasing rate of teenage pregnancy, affect children. In addition to the annual newsletter *Facts at a Glance,* which presents the latest data on teen pregnancy rates for every state, CT also publishes the papers "Next-Steps and Best Bets:

Approaches to Preventing Adolescent Childbearing" and "Welfare and Adolescent Sex: The Effects of Family History, Benefit Levels, and Community Context."

Coalition for Positive Sexuality (CPS)
3712 N. Broadway, PMB #191, Chicago, IL 60613
(773) 604-1654
website: www.positive.org

The Coalition for Positive Sexuality is a grassroots direct-action group formed in the spring of 1992 by high school students and activists. CPS works to counteract the institutionalized misogyny, heterosexism, homophobia, racism, and ageism that students experience every day at school. It is dedicated to offering teens sexuality and safe sex education that is pro-woman, pro-lesbian/gay/bisexual, pro-safe sex, and pro-choice. CPS publishes the pamphlet *Just Say Yes.*

Family Research Council (FRC)
801 G St. NW, Washington, DC 20001
(202) 393-2100 • fax: (202) 393-2134
e-mail: corrdept@frc.org • website: www.frc.org

The council is a research, resource, and education organization that promotes the traditional family, which the council defines as a group of people bound by marriage, blood, or adoption. It opposes schools' tolerance of homosexuality and condom distribution programs in schools. It also believes that pornography breaks up marriages and contributes to sexual violence. Among the council's numerous publications are the papers "Revolt of the Virgins," "Abstinence: The New Sexual Revolution," and "Abstinence Programs Show Promise in Reducing Sexual Activity and Pregnancy Among Teens."

Family Resource Coalition of America (FRCA)

20 N. Wacker Dr., Ste. 1100, Chicago, IL 60606
(312) 338-0900 • fax: (312) 338-1522
website: www.frca.org

FRCA is a national consulting and advocacy organization that seeks to strengthen and empower families and communities so they can foster the optimal development of children, teenagers, and adult family members. FRCA publishes the bimonthly newsletter *Connection,* the report "Family Involvement in Adolescent Pregnancy and Parenting Programs," and the fact sheet "Family Support Programs and Teen Parents."

Focus on the Family

Colorado Springs, CO 80995
(719) 531-5181 • fax: (719) 531-3424
website: www.fotf.org

Focus on the Family is an organization that promotes Christian values and strong family ties and that campaigns against pornography and homosexual rights laws. It publishes the monthly magazine *Focus on the Family* and the books *Love Won Out: A Remarkable Journey Out of Homosexuality* and *No Apologies . . . The Truth About Life, Love, and Sex.*

The Heritage Foundation

214 Massachusetts Ave. NE, Washington, DC 20002-4999
(202) 546-4400 • fax: (202) 546-8328
e-mail: info@heritage.org • website: www.heritage.org

The Heritage Foundation is a public policy research institute that supports the ideas of limited government and the free-market system. It promotes the view that the welfare system has contributed to the problems of illegitimacy and teenage pregnancy. Among the foundation's numerous publications is its Backgrounder series, which includes "Liberal Welfare Programs: What the Data Show on Programs for Teenage Mothers," the paper "Rising Illegitimacy: America's Social Catastrophe," and the bulletin "How Congress Can Protect the Rights of Parents to Raise Their Children."

National Campaign to Prevent Teen Pregnancy

21 M St. NW, Ste. 300, Washington, DC 20037
(202) 261-5655
website: www.teenpregnancy.org

The mission of the National Campaign is to reduce teenage pregnancy by promoting values and activities that are consistent with a pregnancy-free adolescence. The campaign's goal is to reduce the pregnancy rate among teenage girls by one-third by the year 2005. The campaign publishes pamphlets, brochures, and opinion polls that include *No Easy Answers: Research Finding on Programs to Reduce Teen Pregnancy; Not Just for Girls: Involving Boys and Men in Teen Pregnancy Prevention;* and *Public Opinion Polls and Teen Pregnancy.*

National Organization on Adolescent Pregnancy, Parenting, and Prevention (NOAPPP)

2401 Pennsylvania Ave., Ste. 350, Washington, DC 20037
(202) 293-8370
e-mail: noappp@noappp.org • website: www.noappp.org

NOAPPP promotes comprehensive and coordinated services designed for the prevention and resolution of problems associated with adolescent pregnancy and parenthood. It supports families in setting standards that encourage the healthy development of children through loving, stable, relationships. NOAPPP publishes the quarterly *NOAPPP Network Newsletter* and various fact sheets on teen pregnancy.

Planned Parenthood Federation of America (PPFA)

810 Seventh Ave., New York, NY 10019

(212) 541-7800 • fax: (212) 245-1845

e-mail: communications@ppfa.org

website: www.plannedparenthood.org

Planned Parenthood believes individuals have the right to control their own fertility without governmental interference. It promotes comprehensive sex education and provides contraceptive counseling and services through clinics across the United States. Its publications include the brochures *Guide to Birth Control: Seven Accepted Methods of Contraception; Teen Sex? It's Okay to Say No Way;* and the bimonthly newsletter *LinkLine.*

Project Reality

PO Box 97, Golf, IL 60029-0097

(847) 729-3298

e-mail: preality@pair.com

website: www.project-reality.pair.com

Project Reality has developed a sex education curriculum for junior and senior high students called Sex Respect. The program is designed to provide teenagers with information and to encourage sexual abstinence.

Sex Information and Education Council of Canada (SIECCAN)

850 Coxwell Ave., Toronto, ON M4C 5R1 Canada

(416) 466-5304 • fax: (416) 778-0785

e-mail: sieccan@web.net • website: www.sieccan.org

SIECCAN conducts research on sexual health and sexuality education. It publishes the *Canadian Journal of Human Sexuality* and the resource document *Common Questions About Sexual Health Education,* and maintains an information service for health professionals.

Sexuality Information and Education Council of the United States (SIECUS)

130 W. 42nd St., Ste. 350, New York, NY 10036-7802
(212) 819-9770 • fax: (212) 819-9776
e-mail: siecus@siecus.org • website: www.siecus.org

SIECUS is an organization of educators, physicians, social workers, and others who support the individual's right to acquire knowledge of sexuality and who encourage responsible sexual behavior. The council promotes comprehensive sex education for all children that includes AIDS education, teaching about homosexuality, and instruction about contraceptives and sexually transmitted diseases. Its publications include fact sheets, annotated bibliographies by topic, the booklet *Talk About Sex,* and the monthly *SIECUS Report.*

Teen-Aid

723 E. Jackson Ave., Spokane, WA 99207
(509) 482-2868 • fax: (509) 482-7994
e-mail: teenaid@teen-aid.org • website: www.teen-aid.org

Teen-Aid is an international organization that promotes traditional family values and sexual morality. It publishes a public school sex education curriculum, *Sexuality, Commitment and Family,* stressing sexual abstinence before marriage.

Websites

All About Sex

www.allaboutsex.org

This organization encourages teens to feel good about their sexuality. It believes that everyone—regardless of their marital status or sexual orientation—should enjoy and participate in sex. The website offers articles on virginity, sexual intercourse, masturbation, and sexual orientation, among other topics.

Dear Lucie
www.lucie.com

Lucie Walters writes a syndicated newspaper and online advice column for teens called "Adolessons." Her columns discuss incest, sex, sexually transmitted diseases, pregnancy, love and relationships, and health. Visitors to the site can read archives of her columns as well as participate in message boards and chat rooms.

Teen Advice Online
www.teenadviceonline.org

TAO's teen counselors from around the world offer advice for teens on relationships and dating, sex and sexuality, gender issues, Internet relationships, health, family, school, and substance abuse. Teens can submit questions to the counselors or read about similar problems in the archives.

Teenwire
www.teenwire.org

This website was created by Planned Parenthood to provide teens with information about sexuality and sexual health issues. The site offers an online teen magazine, searchable archives, a question-and-answer forum, and informative articles about teen issues.

Whole Family
www.wholefamily.com

This source is designed for both parents and teens. The site's advice columnist, Liz, answers questions about pregnancy, teen sex, drugs, drinking, and body image, while online articles discuss other issues such as divorce, relationships, and health.

Bibliography

Books

Eleanor Ayer

It's OK to Say No: Choosing Sexual Abstinence. New York: Rosen, 1997.

Brent A. Barlow

Worth Waiting For: Sexual Abstinence Before Marriage. Salt Lake City, UT: Deseret, 1995.

George Barna

Third Millennium Teens: Research on the Minds, Hearts, and Souls of America's Teenagers. Ventura, CA: Barna Research Group, 1999.

Ruth Bell

Changing Bodies, Changing Lives: A Book for Teens on Sex and Relationships. New York: Times Books, 1998.

Karen Bouris

The First Time: What Parents and Teenage Girls Should Know About "Losing Your Virginity." Berkeley, CA: Conari Press, 1995.

Marshall Brain

The Teenager's Guide to the Real World. Raleigh, NC: BYG, 1997.

Jack Canfield, Mark Victor Hansen, and Kimberly Kirberger

Chicken Soup for the Teenage Soul: 101 Stories of Life, Love, and Learning. Deerfield Beach, FL: Health Communications, 1997.

Julie K. Endersbe   *Teen Sex: Risks and Consequences.*
                           Mankato, MN: LifeMatters, 2000.

Joshua Harris   *Boy Meets Girl: Say Hello to Courtship.*
                           Sisters, OR: Multnomah Books, 2000.

Joshua Harris   *I Kissed Dating Goodbye.* Sisters, OR:
                           Multnomah Books, 1997.

Nancy Holyoke   *A Smart Girl's Guide to Boys: Surviv-
                           ing Crushes, Staying True to Yourself &
                           Other Love Stuff.* Middleton, WI: Amer-
                           ican Girl, 2001.

Jacqueline Jarosz   *Dating with Confidence: A Teen's Sur-
                           vival Guide.* Holbrook, MA: Adams
                           Media Corp., 2000.

E. James Lieberman   *Like It Is: A Teen Sex Guide.* Jefferson,
and Karen   NC: McFarland, 1998.
Lieberman Troccoli

Stephanie H. Meyer   *Teen Ink: Our Voices, Our Visions.*
and John Meyer, eds.   Deerfield Beach, FL: Health Communi-
                           cations, 2000.

Jill Murray   *But I Love Him: Protecting Your Teen
                           Daughter from Controlling, Abusive
                           Dating Relationships.* New York: Regan
                           Books, 2001.

Jennifer Rozines Roy   *Romantic Breakup: It's Not the End of
                           the World.* Berkeley Heights, NJ: Ens-
                           low, 2000.

Katherine White   *Everything You Need to Know About Relationship Violence.* New York: Rosen, 2001.

Mike Worley   *Forget Me Not: A Youth Devotional on Dating and Relationships.* Euless, TX: Waterbrook Press, 2001.

Periodicals

Rebecca Barry   "Are You Ready for Sex?" *Seventeen,* January 1996.

Bob Bartlett   "Intimacy 101 for Teens," *U.S. Catholic,* August 1999.

Elizabeth Benedict   "Please Touch Me," *Esquire,* September 1997.

Keith Blanchard   "From Here to Virginity," *Sassy,* September 1996.

Jane E. Brody   "Teenagers and Sex: Younger and More at Risk," *The New York Times*, September 15, 1998.

Francesca Delbanco   "The Spin on Teen Sex," *Seventeen*, September 1998.

Tamara Eberlein   "When Your Child's in Love," *Good Housekeeping*, February 1, 1997.

Jill Eisenstadt   "The Virgin Bride," *New York Times Magazine*, June 16, 1996.

Charlotte Faltermayer "Listening In on Boy Talk," *Time*, June 15, 1998.

Gayle Forman   "Sex? No Thanks!" *Seventeen*, August 1999.

Valerie Frankel   "Almost Sex," *Mademoiselle*, October 1996.

Amy M. Holmes   "Hook-Up U," *National Review*, September 13, 1999.

Francine Lavoie   "Teen Dating Relationships and Aggression: An Exploratory Study," *Violence Against Women*, January 2000.

David Lipsky   "Sex on Campus," *Rolling Stone*, March 23, 1995.

Celia Milne   "Sex and the Single Teen," *Maclean's*, December 28, 1998/January 4, 1999.

Christina Nifong   "Teens Learn to Walk Away from Dating Violence," *Christian Science Monitor*, December 16, 1996.

Andrew M. Orosan-Weine "What Parents Need to Know About Dating Violence," *Family and Community Health*, July 1, 1996.

Billy Rayman   "Losin' It! Hey, Guys Are Virgins, Too . . . ," *Sassy*, August 1995.

Robert Rorke   "Coming Out in America," *Seventeen*, April 1999.

Wendy Shalit   "Daughters of the (Sexual) Revolution," *Commentary*, December 1997.

Leora Tanenbaun   "I Was a Teenage Slut," *Ms.,* November/
                         December 1996.

Flora Tartakovsky   "Teen Romance: Many Find Friendship
                         and Sex Without Dating," *Time*, October
                         25, 1999.

Sadie Van Gelder   "It's Who I Am," *Seventeen*, November
                         1996.

Julie Weingarden   "The High Price of Popularity," *Teen*,
                         June 1999.

Daniel B. Wood   "Using Drama to Curb Teen Dating
                         Violence," *Christian Science Monitor*,
                         November 16, 1998.

Index